Classic Sailing-Ship Models in Photographs

R. Morton Nance

DOVER PUBLICATIONS, INC.
Mineola, New York

Bibliographical Note

This Dover edition, first published in 2000, is an unabridged, slightly corrected republication of the work originally published in 1924 by Halton and Truscott Smith, Ltd., London. It includes all 124 numbered plates from the original edition. The full-color frontispiece from that edition is reproduced on the inside front cover.

Library of Congress Cataloging-in-Publication Data

Nance, R. Morton (Robert Morton)
    Classic sailing-ship models in photographs / R. Morton Nance.
        p. cm.
    Previously published: Sailing-ship models. London : Halton and Truscott Smith, 1924.
    ISBN 0-486-41249-0 (pbk.)
    1. Sailing ships—Models—Pictorial works. I. Nance, R. Morton (Robert Morton) Sailing-ship models. II. Title.

VM298 .N36 2000
623.8'201043'0222—dc21

00-034534

Manufactured in the United States of America
Dover Publications, Inc., 31 East 2nd Street, Mineola, N.Y. 11501

CONTENTS

LIST OF PLATES

The author and publishers desire to express their great appreciation of the kindness and courtesy of those who have enabled them to get together the material for this volume and of those whose names appear as having given permission for the inclusion of models owned by them. Special thanks for the trouble they have taken are due, however, to the following:—Mr. G. L. Overton, of the Science Museum, South Kensington; Lieut. Berry, R.N., of the Royal Naval Museum, Greenwich; Colonel H. H. Rogers, Mr. E. E. Kern, Mr. Henry B. Culver and Mr. Clarkson A. Collins, Jr., New York; Mons. Jean Destrem, Conservateur of the Musée de Marine, Paris; Dr. Jules Sottas, Paris; Mr. W. V. Cannenburg, Director of the Netherlands Historical Shipping Museum, Amsterdam; Mr. J. W. Van Nouhuys, Director of the Prins Hendrik Museum, Rotterdam; Rear-Admiral J. Hägg, Superintendent of the State Naval-History Collections, Stockholm; Captain Olof Traung, Director of the Maritime Museum, Gothenburg; Mr. C. E. Aagaard, Press Attaché, Royal Danish Legation, London; and Mr. Einar Lexow, Director of Bergens Museum, Bergen. The author would add to this his thanks for valuable help, not only with material, but with the description of it, given to him by Mr. R. C. Anderson and by Mr. C. E. G. Crone; without making either responsible for the whole, to the former of these may be ascribed the best of the information as to the English models of 1660—1730, and to the latter that concerning Dutch models of a similar period.

SAILING-SHIP MODELS

INTRODUCTION

 HEN comparing the old seafaring with the new, we must all feel that there, by the loss of satisfaction to the eye, we are made to pay dearly for our material gains. Where from the shore one might once have seen an endless stir of ships and boats of all rigs under sail, each of them showing fresh beauties with every change of position as they tacked hither and thither, trimming their canvas to the mood of the wind, and seeming all, with their heeling, gleaming sides, and their cloudy canvas, to have nothing about them that was not as much part of the wind and the sea as the gulls and dolphins that soared or plunged about them; now we have vessels that tack no more, but all go, panting, plodding, or racing, straight on their course, with, it would seem, but one idea possessing them—that of removing their factory-like mechanised masses from an element on which they are desecrations, and as hurriedly as possible returning them to the steel-and-concrete dockside landscapes for which alone their most conspicuous features were planned, and in which only do they look quite at home. Even where sails survive as motive power, present-day ideals are so affected by mechanism that the sailing-ship has become steamer-like in its proportions, its bowsprit becoming shorter and shorter and its masts growing as like one another as a row of telegraph posts; and the dwindling numbers of smaller sailing vessels that still show us seaforms, suggested by the growth of trees and the needs of hemp and canvas, rather than by the standardised production of metal castings, are but survivals from a vanished age.

Each age in turn has had its own reflection at sea in its shipping, and ours could be no exception, but while we have constant proof that sea adventure is not incompatible with plates, castings, rivets, pipes, cranks and levers, turbines, motors, wireless apparatus and the rest, we all feel that this complex hardware is little suggestive of it, and that the romance of the sea is better expressed by the harmony of line and contour that has always been present in the traditional ship, formed of the kindly and tractable timber, hemp, and canvas of tradition, and designed not to ride roughshod over the elements, but to turn them to her service. Failing to find such symbols of sea-life in being, we are naturally driven to seek them more and more in records of the ships that have gone, and of these the most complete that we have are the models that give us not only the one aspect of a pictured ship, but the whole variety of her lines and curves, and the most intimate acquaintance with all her characteristics.

"Sailing-Ship Model" is a term that may describe things as different from one another as the intricate piece of metal-work that on its reduced scale represents a steel-built, wire-rigged five-master and the crude little wooden thing that by a sailor trick of stick-and-string legerdemain is safe harboured, masts on end, in the shelter of a bottle. Between these two extremes—one of them almost too complex for the plain man's enjoyment, the other too simple even for him—there lies a wide field of pleasure open to him in the handiwork of the ship-modellists of several centuries, craftsmen who, taking upon human hands tasks more fit for the finger-tips of fairies, have made for us so many replicas in miniature of ships of all kinds.

Queens among these are those few that survive in which every detail, down to the last bolt or treenail in the hull and the last lashing in the rigging, is exactly as in the original ship, so that to know the model thoroughly is an experience very like that of going over the ship herself. Many are the models that reach this high standard of workmanship as to their hulls, but fewer are so complete as to their rigging, and those that add to these the same perfection of finish in their sails are fewer still. The main reasons for building ship-models of this exact sort were practical ones concerned with the ship-builder's art, and their makers had commonly finished their task when the construction of the hull and its decorations were represented. It is probably true that those features of the ship due to the work of the ship-carpenter and ship-carver are best appreciated in such a model, left mastless, only partially planked, and without the final painting and gilding that hide so much tool-work in the finished vessel; and that being so, masts and sails would seem but superfluities; yet in the finest old English ship-models we often find masts, spars and rigging, everything in fact save sails, added to a hull that exposes its anatomy unplanked, by way of giving as many facts about the ship as can be shown together.

Next to this class of model, which achieves perfect proportion

2

and is in fact a miniature ship, comes a class that has no such practical origin, but represents merely the sailor's love for his ship, and his desire to perpetuate her features as they seem to him to exist. In the best models of this sort we may find a close approximation to true proportion; but as this is dependent on the eye of the model-maker, who in most cases has worked without even so much as a drawing to guide him, it would scarcely be fair to expect it. This is a ship-model for the imaginative mind, perhaps, rather than for the seeker of exact knowledge. Its hull may be "built," after a fashion, but if so its timbers and planking are usually of a very simplified kind, that do not imitate those of the ship herself, and more often its construction is even simpler than this, the whole hull being carved from a single block of wood. Where all the work is done by rule of thumb, its finish depending entirely on the hand and eye of the maker, there is room for many degrees of merit in the result, and while in general truth of representation some of these free-hand models are found to run very close to models made from plans, more of them are clumsy and others are even comically grotesque in their misproportion. Age here may, by adding its own glamour and by softening crudities of colouring, count for much of the charm that such rough work possesses.

In those models that have been made to hang aloft, suspended from the roof of a church or hall, however, a certain misproportion, one cannot help feeling, is more or less intuitive, if not intentional, for it is in all countries invariably of the same kind. The underwater portion of the hull, very often marked off by a wave-line of paint in a style sometimes found on ship's boats, especially whale-boats, of their time, is diminished so that the above-water and more characteristic parts may be more conspicuous when seen from below; and that they may not be lost in viewing them at some distance the details of carved work, blocks, and guns, are all magnified. As in a mediaeval illumination one is prepared to accept the convention of employing different scales in one picture, human interest being represented on one vastly greater than that of castles, ships, or mountains, and kings being twice the size of commoners, so to enjoy the typical church-ship, or even to tolerate it, one must concede to it a similar convention, for to measure it would be as absurd as to compare its figure-head "lion" with a living one at the Zoo. All that one can demand of it (and even that, it must be

3

confessed, it sometimes lacks) is a recognisable likeness to a ship of its time.

Besides these ships of wood and the metal models of metal-built modern ships, we have many ship-models made of materials other than those used for the ships themselves. These cannot be said to be as satisfactory to the ship-lover—usually they are too minute to give one anything very intimate—but they may have their fascination as marvellously fine examples of patient craftsmanship, and even as giving details of ship-building and rigging they are not always to be scorned. Some of the finest of these are made of ivory or of bone. The "prisoner-of-war model," built of saved-up beef-bones that have been laboriously sawn into "timbers" and fastened together with brass pins and most delicately hair-rigged at the expense of the maker's pigtail, even when its proportions leave, as they mostly do, much room for bettering, will always appeal to lovers of historical relics, and one ivory model at least, the silver-rigged *Norse Lion* at Copenhagen (Plate 19), is one of our most valuable records of 17th century shipping. It probably makes little for permanence that a ship, rigging, sails and all, should be cut out of boxwood, as in some exquisitely fine models, yet it may be of service to have rigging thus rendered in less perishable wire, as it is in some others of our oldest models. Silver in itself, too, is a substance of which, in modern times, some fine sailing-ship models have been made, the gleaming sails having quite a pleasing effect, but unfortunately for our knowledge of the earlier ships that might so well have been perpetuated like these in silver, a silversmith's convention that is not yet abandoned, going far beyond that of the church-ship makers, has always preferred "nefs" or "table-ships" of silver or gold of a kind that never were and never could be, so that there is very little to be got from this source. The finest thing of this kind is perhaps the gold cup or "nef" of 1503 (Plate 2), inspired by the carrack print by W̅♉, at Nuremberg. Copper has been used a good deal for the making of weather-vanes in the form of ships, old as well as new; Dordrecht has two 17th-century vanes, a ship and a hoy, gilded, but presumably of copper, and old Dutch pictures show many such, but here again, where we might so easily have had perfect models of ships, we find for the most part mere conventions, scarcely more useful as increasing our knowledge of actual ships than those glass-blown ships with snaky streamers, whose chief claim to our attention is not that they very closely resemble

4

anything, but that they were so difficult to make, and so terribly easy to break. It would be so natural to imitate some actual ship in these things, and is so impossible to produce by ignoring all truth anything but a deformity that is less pleasing to everyone, that one wonders much why such too conventional "ships" should still hold the field. It is easier to understand how they originated centuries ago amongst inland craftsmen who had no opportunities of studying the beautiful balance of parts in any real sailing vessel, and had no W⚓ to copy.

As things of joy, apart from all practical ship-building uses, and all preciousness of material, ship-models have been slow in gaining appreciation, and it is only of late years that their beauty has won them more generally a place that artists have been willing to give them for generations. In studios, indeed, one has long been accustomed to ship-models as a decoration—sometimes painted from, more often enjoyed by their owners simply for their own picturesque qualities—but elsewhere they were rarely seen. "Classical" taste was naturally against them during the 18th century, but the following early nineteenth-century English traveller's description of the Church of St. Nicholas, Boulogne, in days after the "romantic" had displaced the "classical" taste in most things, is worth quoting as showing how little ship-models had gained by the change:—"Before it [the tomb of Admiral Brueys] is suspended from the ceiling a model of a man-of-war dressed up with the flags of all nations. Several other ships are suspended in the same manner in different parts of the church, which make a puerile, paltry appearance . . . . The many paltry paintings, with the tawdry ships before mentioned, render the general view of the inside of the church less imposing than the more chastely adorned church of Calais." This severity is not all intended for the flags, but would certainly include the finest models that could hang there.

Even in the middle of the 18th century it must be admitted that there was some outside appreciation for the more minute work of ship-modellists, at least as "curiosities." In describing the contents of the Royal Museum at Copenhagen, an English traveller, though he is giving but a very brief account of its treasures, finds space to say—"A small man-of-war, in ivory, with silver guns, is a curiosity much admired," referring, of course, to the above-named *Norse Lion* model. Still more enthusiastic is the following description, written in 1767, of a new-made English model as "a very curious little ship of 64 guns, completely rigged, and but four inches long, executed by an officer in the navy," that was presented to the King, who was most graciously pleased to accept of it, "esteeming it worthy of being placed in his royal cabinet of curiosities." The great attractiveness of this model was apparently due to the number of its component materials, "gold, silver, steel, brass, copper, ebony, ivory, hair, &c., the hull, masts, yards, booms, &c., being ivory, the guns, anchors, blocks, deadeyes, &c., silver, the 64 guns weighing but fifty grains; the colours, *viz.*, royal standard, admiralty and union flags, the jack and ensign," it is added, "are also ivory, it is executed on a scale of forty feet to one inch." It is to be feared that those who found such tiny models "admirable for their curiosity" were hardly true model-lovers after all, but would have admired even more a thousand copies of the Lord's Prayer written in the space of a threepenny bit. Kings, as directly interested in things naval, might, without loss of dignity, have such exquisite specimens of ship-models in their cabinets, just as our old friend Captain Cuttle might be allowed to adorn his quarters with coarser examples of the art, but without the excuse of being a ship-owner, a sailor, a sea-painter, or a sea-story writer, one would, until quite recent years, have been thought the possessor of barbarous and eccentric tastes who should dare to decorate his room with such things. As time goes on, however, and the beauty of actual sails, already rare, becomes the unknown thing that it seems likely to be, there is no doubt that lovers of beautiful things will be less and less willing to leave these often wonderfully lovely bits of human handiwork unnoticed.

Perhaps it is mere prejudice, reaction against the glass-shaded monstrosities of the Victorian drawing-room, that still turns many against any form of decoration, always excepting the water-colour painting, that requires the protection of glass. It is at all events a prejudice that must be lived down by the owner of one of those dainty models of the film-and-spillikin kind that one dares not breathe on, and he will have to be reconciled to this vitreous wall between himself and his "princess in the glass coffin," except on the few occasions when, risking damage to his delicate darling, he lets the air in on her for the purpose of taking exact measurements, a photograph or drawing, or a closer view of some detail beneath the magnifying glass. Little can be done to make the case itself a thing of beauty, for any adornment given to case or stand is apt to be at the expense of the model itself, and the glass-sided box is therefore

6

at its best when least obtrusive. This means that, regarded simply as decoration, such exact and delicate specimens of the modellist's art may have to yield to comparatively coarse and clumsy shippikins, that are hardy enough to brave in the open the risks taken by fine pieces of pottery, painting, wood carving or statuary, and to survive an occasional expert dusting with a fine brush and bellows. Hung aloft from the roof in church, hall, or studio, such a ship seems as free of the land as if it floated; placed, almost as well out of danger, on the top of a high cupboard or tallboy it invites to romantic voyages as no glass-cased ship ever could, and taken down and into the open-air the effects of sunlight or moonlight on its sails, the pattern of its shadows, or its reflection in water, even, will give just that admixture of reality and make-believe that is the secret of every aesthetic pleasure, bringing back in another way much of the old glamour that, starting with anything that would float, was able to bring the Indies to a rock-pool on the shore, or the Arctic Regions to a mill-pond. To have made such a model for oneself is ample repayment for the time spent on it; the slow digging out of one's facts, the sacrifice of one's leisure moments, even that monotonous "rattling down" of the shrouds that makes the least exciting part of the work of rigging, weigh as nothing against the comradeship to one's sea-fancies that the finished ship affords as one sets and furls its sails in all possible ways and looks at it from all possible angles. There will be a certain lack, or at least simplification, of detail in such a model, but its happy possessor will be inclined to see even in these deficiencies only another aid to his imagination, and will as easily conjure up the missing touches of its gear as he will raise its elfin crew, or a dream sea on which to set it sailing to Eldorado.

As an inspiration to artists of all kinds, or as a decoration to a room, this super-toy is, perhaps, the ideal ship-model, but it is as a work of art in itself, and not for its suggestiveness, nor for its value in a decorative scheme, that the ship-builder's model demands, and is now receiving, attention. Whether it is the superbly carved, high-sterned ship of the 17th century, or whether it evidences the more restrained taste in ship-architecture of another age, it is not merely as a record of past fashions, but as a beautiful bit of handiwork and a miniature copy of the graces of the vanished ship herself that such a model is valued.

In every country the best skill obtainable has always been lavished upon the carved work of ships, and in the 17th century especially no sculptor or painter seems to have thought it beneath his dignity to design allegorical decorations to finish the work of ship-builders. Sometimes, indeed, the greatness of the sculptor was a danger to the ship thus honoured, as when in France Puget grew too exuberantly florid with his rococo high-relief statues and had to be restrained by the firm practical hand of d'Almeras or of Colbert, or, as when given too free a hand on a " ship royal," earlier artists elsewhere added a superfluity of too ornate galleries, embrasures and turrets to what without them had been handsomer ships; for the most part, however, the designers of such work seem to have had an excellent eye for the lines of a ship, and they make the carved work blossom forth from these flowing curves as naturally and inevitably as a flower grows from its stalk or a foam-crest curls from a billow.

It is this justness of design, very largely the result of keeping to conditions imposed by nature, but also the result of profiting by tradition, that makes the beauty of a decorated ship, and we may be very sure that the grander beauty of the hull unadorned was quite appreciated by the artists who have in almost every case added just the final touches of enrichment that give expression to its lines. Thus the ornate ship of 1660 was not merely the ship of 1760, plus a great deal of unnecessary and foppish carving, but the comparatively large amount of decoration had an exact relation to her greater sheer and to her greater height astern, and all of these were diminished together, the difference in decoration between the ship of 1760 and that of 1860 being of exactly the same kind. As there is nothing of man's creation that so closely resembles a living organism as does a sailing ship, so in a series of ships of different periods we have the closest approach to a scale of evolution in organic life that is made by anything inanimate.

There are two ways of looking at most things, and the evolution of the ship is no exception. We may, if we choose, see in it a movement towards perfection, at first slow, but latterly very rapid, that culminated with the arrival of the 19th-century clipper ship; the whole scale between *Noah's Ark* and *Cutty Sark* being filled with a series of imperfect ships, less and less clumsy as time advances, but all ineffective attempts at reaching clipper standard. If we adopt this clipper-man's view of ship-evolution we should be prepared to carry it further. The wooden clipper will then but herald the iron ship, and that the steel. The clipper's square-rig sail plan, too, will have to yield to the more advanced arrangement of seven-masted schooners, and in the end all sailing vessels must be treated as the result of abortive attempts at finding out the "right" (i.e., the most advanced) method of driving a ship through the water by mechanical means. Leaving ships, we should have, on this principle, to condemn all forms of handwriting, including the triumphs of the mediaeval illuminator's art with the fine flourished hands of his successors, as clumsy strivings after the perfections of the printing-press and the typewriter; all architecture might lead up to the reinforced-concrete skyscraper, or the graphic arts all end in the cinema. This "whatever is is best" view of evolution in the arts, that for the time ends everywhere in something mechanical, will not please the antiquarian, the artist, and the craftsman, and to others as well, it will, I believe, seem more reasonable to look for many states of "perfection" in the course of ship-evolution, most of which, like that of the clipper-ship, have been reached only to be abandoned in the search for another. We may then take a ship of any given age or country as being a sea-expression of the ideals, social and artistic, of that age; often arriving at a finish and poise that may well be called perfection, but ever changing as some newly desired convenience was secured that necessitated a new adjustment of its nicely balanced parts. There must, all through the history of shipping, have been time after time when old sailors, grown used to a settled and "perfect" ship, thought that innovators were ruining the beauty of ships for ever with their new fangles; and in pictures, too, we often find that artists have refused to acknowledge any recent change or addition, preferring ships "as they ought to be."

To look back no further than to the great sail-less rowing-boat of the North, known to us by a specimen dug up at Nydam—its broad keel still showing how it started as a dug-out, its ribs lashed in after the planks were fitted to keel and stems, its bow and stern alike, so that it was always ready to be rowed straight away from the beach, needing nothing in preparation save a re-tying of its reversible rowlocks—one finds that in this a perfection of symmetry had been reached which cannot but have been marred for those who had grown used to it by the addition to it of a mast and sail, and the consequent differentiation in it of bow from stern.

Acquiring poise anew, once the shock of change has passed, we get the noble simplicity of the one-sailed Norse ship of the Viking Age, with its soaring stem and stern-post that carried the curving lines of the sheer straight heavenward, to end in axe-hewn carvings symbolic of all that a ship meant to the men of that day—a sea-steed, a serpent, a dragon. What a destruction of this beauty and imagery it must have seemed when box-like fighting-castles, bad enough when temporarily raised inboard as "stages," far worse, were made to cut across all the gathering together of the curves at bow and stern with permanent platforms and parapets, repeated on a smaller scale even at the masthead, all having no relation to the ship as a ship, but emphasising, on the contrary, a new distinction between seaman and fighter, and putting the latter in all senses higher up.

Yet again a new poise was found, and the "castles" assimilated only to be disturbed when seamen found themselves condemned to the indignity of having to steer with a rudder that, instead of being slung on the "steer board," where as everyone knew a rudder should be, was made by a most lubberly contrivance to hang, as one can fancy them saying, "wagging to-and-fro on hinges, like any door on land," and that moreover from the stern-post, whereby the clean-ended appearance of the ship was ruined.

It is not long before we arrive at a new type of ship on which any other rudder would look absurd, and the next thing to horrify the "old sailor," who perhaps had taken the innovation of adding trivial-seeming little fore, top and mizen masts and sails more quietly, is the blunt chopping off, astern, of all the graceful gathering-in of the planking that he had been used to, and the substitution for it of the "square-tuck" stern that was characteristic of the 16th century.

In the same way portholes, when first cut for guns, must surely have seemed defacements of a ship's smooth flanks; again when through the 17th and 18th centuries the swinging curves of a vessel's sheer, the narrow loftiness of her stern, the profusion of her carved work, and the simplicity of her sail-plan, were becoming less with each modification of design, many must have thought sadly of the days in which "ships looked like ships," and when these modifications had at last resulted in the new perfection of a ship as nearly as possible without sheer, without carving, and with batteries emphasised at the expense of form by their straight lines of "magpie" black-and-white paint, still more must have pined for the bright gilding and the shapely yellow topsides of older fleets. This is not merely to say that there have always been grumblers at every new thing, for in every one of these changes there was a real disturbance of an achieved poise, and a destruction, usually with some desirable practical object, of an achieved perfection. Each time, an innovation was to lead to a new type, in itself perhaps as beautiful, sometimes even more beautiful, than the old; but, as first introduced, it was apt to be merely destructive of beauty.

The steady improvement in the ship, regarded merely as a sure, swift, and economical sailing-machine, during this period shows that through the centuries, from the 15th to the 19th, there were certain minds that were not willing to leave things as they found them, yet to the average sailor the average ship of his day has always seemed good enough. If his was not a speedy ship, perhaps it was a dry one. If it refused to sail as near the wind as some others, perhaps it outpaced these when going free, and the main thing was that it should look as a ship ought to look, and behave in the way that a ship should behave, without unduly upsetting the traditions in these things.

As we none of us set great value on a ship-model as a means of speedy or efficient navigation, but care most that it should satisfy the eye, our own way of regarding these may be much the same, each in its turn being considered by us as a finished expression of the taste of its own age as manifested in the building, decorating and rigging of ships. In the ship of a given period we shall then see something that is all of a piece, not only with its land architecture, but with its costume, and its manners. Thus, in an Elizabethan ship, we shall not only see the expected mixture of Gothic with classical in its strap-work ornament, its balustrades and turrets, but we shall be reminded by its jaunty open gallery and beak-head of the be-ruffled and courtly dandy in trunk-hose that bestrode its deck, and as a final touch the outlicker astern will even repeat for us the effect of the up-tilted rapier that sticks out from beneath his velvet cloak. Similar resemblances between ships of the Restoration period, with their flowing curves and elaborate carving, to cavaliers in feathers, lace and periwigs, to the gabled houses that they lived in, the high-backed chairs that they sat in—even to their flourished handwriting—are obvious enough, and even more is the 18th century written all over the mouldings and pilasters of the stern of a ship of 1750, or early Victorian ideals reflected in a frigate of 1850. If we connect the tubular bridge, tubular coat-sleeves, hats, and trouser-legs, with the tubular funnel and the semi-cylindrical paddle-box of the contemporary steamer and see this rule-and-compass ideal of beauty in simplicity producing a round-countered stern on sailing ships, or if in contemplating the expansion of feminine crinoline at the expense of human semblance we are reminded of the expansion of canvas in clippers and yachts until the hull becomes relatively a mere straight line on the water, we shall easily go on to find such analogies through all the ages and read the mind of a people in its ships and boats perhaps even better than in its land buildings. When once we begin to do this, such an anachronism as a jib on a Roman galley will seem as poor a piece of fun as a " bowler" on the brow of Caesar, and we should no more give the *Santa Maria* a bob-stay than we should portray Columbus in a bob-wig.

In a ship of any given time, as in the life, language, or dress of the community to which it belongs, we find traditional survivals of things past, and prophetic foreshadowing of things to come, so that no one ship can ever be understood if considered apart from all others, yet we find as we know them better, not only that those of one period have the character that belongs to that period alone, or that there is a certain expression imparted by each rig to the vessel that wears it, but that each ship or boat has an individuality, more or less marked, that is quite its own. Dignity or impudence, innocence or guile, heartiness, cruelty, openness, stealth, determination, flightiness, every quality that is embodied in man, woman, bird, beast or fish, is expressed not only in ship names, but also in ship forms. The rakish pirate schooner and the beamy old Dutch buss of the Dogger Bank, ship for ship, are as contrasted as are their skippers, man for man—the swaggering pirate, lean and swarthy, armed to the teeth; the fisherman, rosy-cheeked and round as a herring-barrel, comfortably smoking his long pipe. The long, low, black-sided clipper, gleaming with gun-muzzles and crowded with canvas; the herring-buss, round-sterned, apple-bowed, and snug, not so much as a bowsprit to dandify her, riding to her nets while the caboose smoke-pipe makes promise of dinner. These are but two extreme types, but they emphasise the point, that a sailing ship is an expression of human thought and feeling—in fact, a true work of art. And if this is true of a ship, it is no less true of a ship-model, made for the pure love of ship-form and ship-character, and without even the ship-builder's care for any lower consideration of practical utility.

12

As an art depending on the working together of hand and eye, no doubt the ship-builder's work was at its highest pitch before the invention of saw or plane, for in those days each man needed an artist's skill in the use of axe or adze, and an artist's understanding of his material. Every piece of timber in the ship had been, after due seasoning, picked for its own place, in each was some particular quality of grain or texture that made it the right one, and the dressing-down given it by the well-sharpened tool was to the axe-wielder like the reading of a book, so much was there to be learned about it in the process. We have still existing in the Gokstad and other Viking ships evidence of the wonderful work that was turned out by such old-fashioned, rule-of-thumb methods, and there is no reason to suppose that work as excellent was not turned out by the old Mediterranean builders long before them. When theory and science took over the traditional master ship-builder's work, and invention brought quicker ways of obtaining results, a certain amount of the old instinct for timber-construction and accuracy of eye and hand were lost, but enough of them remain to make common boat-building still a fine thing, even to watch, and the older ship-models, made by men whose names even are rarely known, but that show these old qualities to the full, though in miniature, are things that almost defy imitation.

Most amateur ship-modellists, aware that from the minute accuracy, the exact knowledge, and the endless patience that they demand, such built models are not for them, are content to carve their hulls, acknowledging that were life long enough they would do otherwise. They can make no claim to inherit the ship-builder's art, but theirs, too, is a very ancient craft, not only as imitating the log-hollowing of old, but as following a time-honoured tradition of model-making.

THE GROWTH OF THE SHIP-MODELLER'S ART.

HE tiny, imitative art of ship-modelling, like the great creative arts, had its first beginnings in rites, half magical, half religious, by which man sought to control his fate, or groped his way towards a working theory of the universe, and is probably as old as the art of navigation itself.

The setting afloat of rude models of boats as offerings to the spirits, demons, or gods that control river-currents or sea-storms, with hope thereby to avert their attention from the boats themselves, is a rite that one might expect to find practised by the holders of any primitive faith, and one finds survivals of this not only in far parts of the earth, where such little vessels are still launched, but also it may be in places much nearer home, where, as in West Cornwall and in Guernsey, Good Friday of all days in the year is one on which every fisher-boy observes a traditional custom of sailing his toy-boat, giving a strong suggestion that the custom is a survival from days when a general propitiatory sacrifice of miniature boats heralded the opening of the season of seafaring.

Such boat offerings may well have been sent on Nile-appeasing voyages down the stream, but in Ancient Egypt it is as tomb-furniture that we still have ship-models preserved to this day. These again were connected with religious belief, for they were left buried with the owner of the original vessel so that from their lines might be built another fit for his needs in the spirit-world. Some of these Egyptian models, although block-carved, are finished with considerable detail, as notably one, perhaps the best, that came from the tomb of Mehenkwetre, Chancellor of Egypt about two thousand years B.C., and is now in the Metropolitan Museum, New York, which shows not only the crew, one steering, another heaving the lead, but also the mast and sail, the latter with all its rigging, including its boom below with the many standing lifts, just as we find these in contemporary wall-paintings and sculptures, the whole giving quite a satisfactory idea of accuracy. It is not in the nature of man to put his best work where it is not to be subjected to the criticism of his living fellow-man, and just as any rough suggestion of a boat was held good enough for fobbing off a boat-wrecking demon, so as

14

MODEL FROM TOMB OF MEHENKWETRE

provision for the future life of great Egyptians a scamped rough-sketch of a model was commonly made to serve. In such propitiatory or substituted models we may perhaps look for the origins of toy-boats, and so of model yachts, but it seems likely that it was rather as votive offerings, open acknowledgments of supernatural aid, made by the christened to be seen of their even-Christians, by the heathen to be seen by fellow-pagans, and displayed in places of worship, that the more complete portraits of ships, the true ancestors of our own ship-models, were first made.

Votive junks, highly-finished portrait-models, are still exposed in Chinese temples, just as in European churches we find hanging church-ships old and new, and a custom that is thus found at the most widely separated points of the Old World may well be thought to have its roots very deep in the past. In Jutland, whence a church-ship, that of sand-buried Old Skja- gen, makes its appear-

VOTIVE BOATS OF GOLD, JUTLAND

15

ance in literature—coming down from the roof and sailing away as large as life, in a tale of Hans Christian Andersen's—and where the church-ship is still an institution, a peat-bog has yielded three conventionally shaped votive boats of gold that date back to the first century; but boats and ships of pottery, apparently votive offerings, that go back very much farther than this, have been dug up in Amathus, Cyprus, and Carthage. All through the Middle

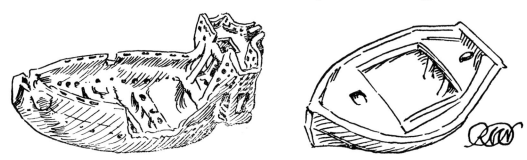

VOTIVE SHIPS OF POTTERY, AMATHUS AND CARTHAGE

Ages we have reason to assume that any church attended by seafarers, whether by profession or as pilgrims, would have been likely to have had its *ex voto* ship or ships. Now and then we have an actual record of them, as at Bristol, where in the 15th century the chapel of St. Anne had twenty-seven votive models of wood, to which no monetary value was attached, and five of silver, valued at twenty shillings apiece.

In the Middle Ages, and long after, things that were old were only things to be despised, and worm-eaten models of wood were doubtless pulled down and burnt, and silver models melted down into new shapes, so that the thank-offerings of the living might replace those of the forgotten dead. This alone would account for the total loss of all those one-masted "nefs," "barges," "balingers" and "cogs," with their fore, top, and after "castles," the details of which would have so well eked out those too grudgingly given by conventional seals and yet more conventional monk-made miniatures.

Veneration for relics other than saintly is a sentiment far too modern to have saved us any of these, and even without wilful destruction at times of rebuilding or cleaning, models of their kind could not greatly have outlived their makers. To begin with, they were carved from blocks of wood, but slightly lightened as a rule by hollowing, and were of considerable weight, so that it is easy to imagine that a damp church, by rotting ropes, or

16

rusting wires and chains, might have brought disaster to ships themselves as well as to possible worshippers beneath. Even failing such a downfall, their soft-wood " cage-work " and spars, their inferior cordage, and their thinly distemper-painted hulls themselves, were by no means proof against the attacks of time, so that a bare fifty years might thus seem a fair average of endurance for them.

In those countries that accepted the Reformation one might expect that *ex voto* church-ships, as having been offered in gratitude, usually either to Our Lady or to St. Nicholas, the sailors' patron, should have been condemned wholesale as " superstitious," and in England and Scotland this seems to have happened, for from that time we hear practically nothing of such models in these countries; but even this is doubtful, for in Lutheran countries, where the church-ship became commemorative rather than votive, as in Catholic countries where votive church-ships are still countenanced, although they remain as a traditional institution, we are no luckier in finding anything earlier than the 16th century, and very little that is as early.

Although they have long since gone to warm the sexton's chimney-corner, lost church-ships may have left traces of their existence in the better-drawn ships of miniaturists and seal-engravers. It was, I am sure, a church-ship that inspired the finest drawing that we have of a 15th-century ship—the *kraeck*, of the Flemish engraver who signs himself W♄. In the first place, this engraver has given full proof in other prints, five of smaller ships, " barges," one of a herring-buss, and one of a line-fishing hooker, that he had slight knowledge of rigging, proving that the carrack's wealth of detail was not drawn from memory. Again, the hull is shown impossibly high out of the water, and is given scanty underwater parts, both suggesting that she was drawn not from a ship but from a church-ship model, a suggestion borne out by the over-large blocks, bored but sheaveless, the twisted-wire fastenings of the lower dead-eyes, and lastly the curious fact that, although otherwise rigged to the final detail, ropes as important to a real ship as the ties and halyards, by which the yards are raised or lowered, are left out. The reason why church-ships should so almost universally have bored blocks only is obvious—sheaves show but little, and would give ten times the work; the same applies to the substitution of a twisted wire for the difficult metal-work detail of the chains, and to a model-maker (who must in these old ships remember

17

to fix his knight-head down below and reeve his halyards through this and the ram-head *before he finally fixes his deck*, if he means to rig ties and halyards at all) it is very clear that the absence of this important gear, so often left out in old church-ships, points to a ship-model as original of the picture.

Of three other vessels, two carracks and a galley, in a painting by Carpaccio (Plate 1), there is no question as to their church-ship origin, for they are painted, surrounded by other votive offerings, as features in a church interior. With this hint, it becomes possible to trace back to a similar origin others among Carpaccio's ships, for it is not unusual to find these represented as floating rather unnaturally high out of the water, and with blocks on a scale that makes them too conspicuous. A 16th-century print, representing a philosopher

HANGING MODEL IN A PHILOSOPHER'S STUDY

in his study, gives us, with his books and spheres, another little hanging ship that is an early example of the " lay " model, though hardly different enough from the church-ship to be claimed as a ship-builder's. This is enough to show that artists who were fond of painting shipping subjects might, even in Carpaccio's day, have had little ships of their own, and that they were, even thus early, not peculiar to churches; but with the 16th century we find not pictures only, but actual models.

18

If we may judge by appearances alone, the *doyen* of this company is a model from the collection of the late Sir William Van Horne (Plate 4), which is either a church-ship of about 1525 or a forgery of one so skilful as to deserve a high place as a "reconstruction." Unfortunately it comes to us without a pedigree, and worse still, after passing through the hands of curio-dealers who were not above tinkering with old models nor even innocent of offering the most bare-faced of "fakes." The rigging, if original, has clearly been tampered with, and its disorder is not necessarily a sign of great age, but it would seem unlikely that a forger should have the knowledge requisite to give the hull of his ship just this combination of high forecastle and narrow, sheering, three-countered poop; round stem and square-tuck stern, and not only to place the guns rightly, and add just the right contemporary touch of herring-bone pattern in the painting, but to render all these characteristic features with exactly the disproportion of above-water detail to underbody that has always distinguished the church-ship. Still more in its favour is its freedom from any attempt at the carving by which ship-model forgers attempt to give interest and value to their productions. It has not even a figure-head, and, speaking as strongly for it as this reticence in decoration, we find under the lower counter two quite unromantic garderobe vents, of unusual form, but not unlike those of the ship in a window at King's College Chapel, Cambridge, and at all events placed just where they would be in such a ship. The fender-bolts with which it is studded also seem possible enough. If only to invite further criticism, it seems at all events worth while to draw attention to this unvouched-for model, which is certainly not based on any known contemporary painting; for if genuine it is a valuable record, and if proved a "fake" may be as useful a warning.

A rival to this is an ancient model in the Naval Museum at Venice, that has there been accepted as representing a Venetian *cocca* or "cog" of the 15th century, as then employed in the Flanders trade. In its present form it is more possible as a ship of the first half of the 16th century, but from the shape of its stern can hardly be earlier, and it has apparently suffered rather drastic "restoration," to which possibly it owes the exaggerated forefoot that seems so little characteristic of ships of its reputed age. Another model at Venice (Plate 5) is a little later in date, being of the fashion of about 1550-1560, but shows a very convincing likeness to

19

the ship-pictures of that date. Although she has been called a *galeone*, she has not the lower beak-head, imitating that of a galley, that marks the 16th-century galleon, but retains the old, ship-style, projecting forecastle of earlier centuries in a but slightly modified form, and should, I think, rather be called a *nave* or ship. A drawing made from this very interesting model by Jal in 1835 shows that her wire rigging has since then been "restored" by someone who has tried to improve on the original arrangement, the braces in particular having now a less correct lead, and bobstays being added, as in the "cocca." Jal also shows the topsail-yards hoisted higher, as though sails might once have been set on them, and in his time we find that the mizen-yard and the broadside guns were lacking, and that a "ram-head" block was still attached to the ties of the main-yard, but twisted round so as to come before the main-mast. The crosses at the mast-heads (two in Paris's picture of her, *Souvenirs de Marine*, III.) are not shown by Jal, and a bulkhead and ladder at the poop are new also; otherwise the little ship is just as she was in 1835, and not very different from what she was when new.

That models of equal accuracy and even fuller detail were by 1550 being made in the Netherlands one might easily guess, but I think we may safely go further than this, and in two of the shipping plates engraved by Frans Huys, after drawings by Pieter Bruegel the elder, discover carefully-made portraits of one of these. Bruegel, in drawing others of his ships, may have found church-ships useful,

THREE SHIPS DRAWN BY BRUEGEL FROM A MODEL

20

but here we find what looks like proof that he did, for in one plate he gives us a broadside view of a ship with an unusually tall mizen-mast, furled sails, and yards all set a-cock-bill, in what has long been mourning-garb for ships, canted down to starboard on the foremast, to port on the mainmast; and when we find that the next plate gives us three ships, two of which are bow and stern views of this very ship in every detail, down to the exact cock of the yards, remembering the headlong imagination of this artist in his common mood, it is almost impossible not to see in this repetition evidence that it was here restrained by close attention to a model. That an actual ship was not drawn from is strongly suggested by the way in which these three ships are set in the water, as well as by the fact that they are given quite different land-backgrounds. Artists have in later times gained courage to attempt painting moving vessels after practice on the "still-life" of models, and it is not at all unlikely that the skill in ship-painting for which Dutch painters, beginning with Pieter Bruegel, gained so well-earned a fame was in part due to the ease with which they could find church-ships to study.

In 1571 all Christendom was rejoicing over the check given to the Turk at Lepanto, and many must have been the votive galleys or galeasses offered by survivors of the fight; but of these nothing remains. One reminder of their existence we do find, though, in a rough woodcut that illustrates Bartolomeo Crescentio's *Nautica Mediterranea* of 1607, and instead of representing a galeass of that date, closely resembles the six galeasses of Venice that took part in the battle of Lepanto. She has not only the semicircular turret forecastle and ram beak, the guns over the oars, three lateen yards, and Noah's-Ark-like deck-cabin aft, of these vessels as pictured, but is obviously drawn straight from a rather roughly made church-ship model that had already had time to get somewhat out of order, the sails having departed from the main and mizen yards, and the latter having lost its controlling "orses" and "ostes," so that one need have little hesitation in claiming this as a Lepanto *ex voto*.

As much as Lepanto in Venice, an occasion for thanksgiving and commemoration in England and Holland was the Armada fight of 1588, but of this, too, not a single church-ship record survives. This is not to say, though, that no ship-model was made in honour of the victory, for one, of the little *Francis of Fowey*, of 140 tons and 60 men, a volunteer with the Lord Admiral under command of her owner, John Rashleigh, hung long in the hall of the Rashleigh

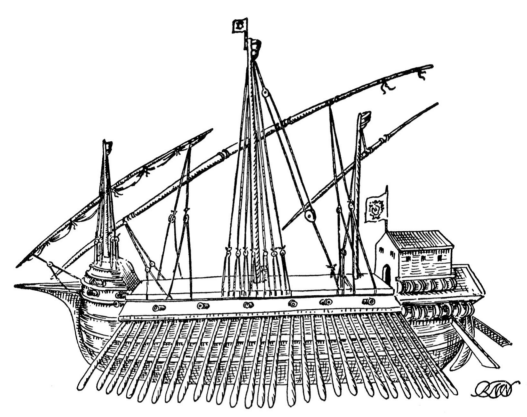

LEPANTO VOTIVE GALEASS FROM CRESCENTIO (*See p. 21*)

mansion at Fowey, in Cornwall. Hals, in his rare history of the county, published in 1750, describes this as "a small ship formed by a ship-carpenter, of timber, with masts, sails, ropes, guns and anchors, and figures of men thereon, which is hung up to the roof with an iron chain in their old house in this town, of which those gentlemen have often given me ocular observation." The old house became later the "Ship Inn," so called from the *Francis*, which despite this change, still hung there. Still later it was taken down from its chain, and, as a more fitting position, given place above the last resting-place of John Rashleigh in Fowey Church, with an iron rail to defend it from over-busy fingers. It paid dearly in the end for the dignity of preferment to church-ship rank, for at one of those devastating "restorations" it was cast out and burnt before John Rashleigh's descendants knew of its danger, and of it nothing remains but a uselessly crude little woodcut showing its former position in the church, and the words of description to add to those of Hals, that it was "raised at stem and stern," showing that either

22

its extreme sheer or its raised poop and forecastle distinguished it at once from 19th-century ships.

Another little ship that may well belong to the end of the 16th century is now at the Trinity House at Leith (Plate 8). Its history is a blank, but if a late 16th-century church-ship is not an impossibility in Scotland one might hazard a guess that it celebrated the national thanks for the safe return to Scotland, after long delays caused by witch-raised storms, and many months spent in Norway and Denmark, of James VI., with his bride, Anne of Denmark. The date of this, 1590, fits the ship well enough, and the one tradition about her connects her with Mary of Guise, bride of James V., which, though too early, is at least a royal marriage; strongest point of all, though, is that she is a great Danish ship, with two turreted galleries, and bears on her taferel the crowned C embracing a 4 that was the monogram of King Christian IV. of Denmark, Anne's brother. From the beginning of his reign this sailor monarch is known to have attracted Scottish ship-builders like Balfour and Sinclair to his yards; but this is not a shipwright's model. On the contrary, it is an extreme example of church-ship exaggeration, and the fact that it has been carefully rigged anew at the beginning of the 18th century hints that it was honoured as a church-ship even at that time. This, too, in Britain, not in Denmark, if such details of the rigging as caps and topsail-sheet blocks witness truly.

Even more incongruously re-rigged, in a caricature of early 19th-century style, is a ship at the Bergen Museum, that for centuries hung in the Church of St. Mary at that place (Plate 14). Bearing an image of Our Lady on its stern, it was probably made especially for this church, to which it is to be restored. Though reputed to be a Hanseatic Bergen-trader, it seems likely to be an emblem of sea-power rather than a portrait, and to show the maker's ideal of the finest possible ship, perhaps again, one of the Danish Navy under Christian IV. With its two roofed-in close-galleries, its turrets and its many guns, it would be, at all events, a great ship of its day (which must be just beyond 1600) and one more adapted for war than trade, even when that might imply fighting one's way to business as part of the venture. With Möller's engraving of a Danish ship of 1600 as a guide, it would be easy to restore to this its old rig.

A model of the end of the 16th century of which we have a

23

little more knowledge is one in the Naval Museum at Madrid (Plates 9 and 10). This is a rather conventional representation of a "ship royal," ideal rather than actual, though it is full of good detail, that was made in Flanders, and sent by loyal subjects there as a gift to Philip II. of Spain. In 1838, the artist Don Valentin Carderera made a sketch of this ship, then in the Armeria, which Jal reproduces in woodcut form in his *Glossaire Nautique*. He gives but a poor idea of the very elaborate painting that covers the ship, and one band of pattern, that represents appropriately the linked steel "strike-a-lights" of the collar of the Order of the Golden Fleece, is not in his picture. He scarcely does justice, either, to the details of the carving in the delicate foliated scroll-work of the long gallery and the very unshiplike band of carved fretwork enriched with filigree that runs forward from the gallery to the fiddle-head of the beak. An interesting Flemish inscription runs along between the guns of the lower tier, beginning at the port bow :—

"ICK VARRE MET NEPTUNUS EN BOREAS HULPENCHE

TOT DIE HAVEN DAER MI ANKER VALT. ANO 1593 "

"I sail with Neptune and Boreas' help, to that haven where my anchor falls. Anno 1593." Carderera makes the lettering run the wrong way and misreads this date as 1523, a mistake not corrected by Jal, and he was not interested in the rigging, satisfying himself with the masts and tops. The wrong date is easily put right, but the rigging in 1838 must have been in better condition than we now find it, and it is tantalizing to have missed this so narrowly. Although offered to man, mortal though royal, as a symbol of sea-power and no *ex voto,* this ship was perhaps meant to hang, with anchors dropped, for in its proportions it follows church-ship conventions; an inscription, even, is not unknown in such models, for one is conspicuous on the white paint beneath a North Frisian church-ship as painted in an interior by Ludwig Dettmann, and the same thing, though much hidden in our view of it, occupies the same place on a 17th-century church-ship that comes from Flensburg (Plate 38).

A church-ship, dated 1603, and in its original condition as to hull, though re-rigged in 1715, and again in 1822, when a crew was added, is in the Germanic National Museum, Nuremberg (Plate 11). This has the open gallery carved from the solid block, but is full of good detail and would thoroughly repay for a third restoration of a more scientific kind.

Of all church-ships the most famous are probably those that

hang in the Groote Kerk of St. Bavo at Haarlem (Plates 1 and 15). These commemorate the capture of Damietta in Egypt, the ancient Pelusium (and also the name-place of the fabric "dimity"), after a siege, in which William I., Count of Holland, distinguished himself; ended, tradition says, by a Dutch ship that cut the harbour-chain which closed the port, by running at it with a saw-armed prow. This was in the fifth crusade, in 1219 to be exact, but though the clock-chimes—the *Damiaatjes*—that hang in the church tower are said, with what truth I know not, to be one actual thank-offering of Count William, we are not to suppose that the ships are another. They are quite likely, though, to be the latest links in a chain of ships that goes back as far, for a folk-custom of making procession through Haarlem streets in memory of Damietta was kept for centuries by children who, as they marched, carried little ships fixed upon sticks. The present models, a hoy with a lateen mizen, and two full-rigged ships with saw-armed stems, are of the 17th century. The hoy and the larger ship, which is shown in the act of cutting, with its saw, the chain slung between two suspended castles of "Damietta Haven," were made to the order of the Great Guild of Skippers, or Shipmasters, in 1686, and the smaller ship was, one can see, a good deal re-rigged at the same date. She is actually between sixty and seventy years older though, as is shown by her longer beak, her high, narrow poop, her greater sheer, and her open gallery astern. She also has the grating over the waist, the deep round-tops, caps open before and topmast lashed to the lower-mast head, with the characteristic heart-shaped deadeyes and outside chains of this earlier period. This must therefore have been one of the "two models of ships, completely equipped, in memory of that invention of saws under their keels, with which they cut through the chain of booms, which barred the port of Damietta" that John Evelyn saw hanging there in 1641. Huet, the rhyming traveller, who, on his Tour to Stockholm, was at Haarlem in 1652, mentions as the most famous sight there, "the ships with saw-like prows, fatal to their Pelusian foes," as his words are Englished. The Dutch naval architect, Witsen, writing in 1671, and a little astray with his history though no doubt following tradition, says, "The ship hangs displayed in the church at Haarlem even to this day which, in 1190, under command of Diederik, seventh Count of Holland, opened the harbour at Damietta with a saw at the bottom of the keel, that cut the iron chain by which it was closed." Both Evelyn and Witsen

25

thus mention a saw-armed keel, and not a saw-armed prow, as described by Huet and as seen in the surviving pre-1689 model, as an attribute of at least one of these older ships. Evelyn visualized a wooden boom cut through by a keel driven over it, and Witsen, who knew well enough what ships of 1620 or so were like, seems to have disregarded the saw-prowed survivor, noticed by Huet, to concentrate attention on a saw-keeled ship that he believed to be a contemporary model of 1190. This ship, we may be sure, must have been of considerable antiquity, though, had it survived, we might have had to refuse to give it as he did to 1190, or even to 1219.

Furttenbach's *Architectura Navalis*, 1629, like Crescentio's book, records in its illustrations some models that have ceased to exist. His galleys suggest drawings from an elaborately finished scale model, but his square-rigged ship is unmistakably copied from a rather clumsy church-ship, with over-heavy spars and blocks. A "Turkish

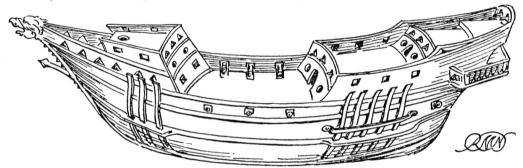

16th CENTURY MODEL, FURTTENBACH

carramuzzal " that he gives is more interesting than either of these, because, quite unlike a caramuzzal, which was a small, moon-sheered, high-sterned, and ketch-rigged vessel, it represents a mastless model of a full-rigged ship of about 1550-60, armed with a ram beneath its beak-like projecting fore-castle, such as is shown in several contemporary pictures.

With the coming of the middle of the 17th century, we reach many more actual church-ships that have survived, but two that hang in the Town Hall at Bremen (Plate 16), one of about 1625, the other perhaps twenty years later, serve as links between these and the few older models. To the period between 1650 and 1700 belong a number of the models in the Hall of the Guild of Shipmasters at Lübeck (Plates 26 and 40), and one that hangs in the Town Hall at Emden (Plate 16), besides several others in Holland, Denmark, Norway and Sweden, and at least one Italian church-ship

26

"DE MAEGT VAN GHENDT," 1672

from Genoa. One at Bruges, named "The Virgin of Ghent," and bearing her image on her stern, is remarkable for its unusually good carving, dated 1672, though the ship itself is not a very possible one, and has the open galleries and beak design of an earlier date. Although most of these are of the true church-ship type, block-carved, and clumsy as to detail, wavy as to water-line, and scanty beneath it, we begin to find at this time votive and symbolical or commemorative models that are, if not built to scale, at least roughly put together with oversized planking upon a timber frame, and in

27

such models we find often a neatness of workmanship in the rigging that causes the free folk-art of church-ship making to merge into the more exacting art of professional ship-modelling. Yet, through a long succession of church models, the older methods have survived, as being within the means of the little-skilled, and in Provençal, Norman or Breton churches, as in those of Holland, North Germany, Denmark, Norway or Sweden, this crude block-carved model is still the rule. Two notable modern exceptions to this are a fine reconstruction of Niels Juel's ship, *Christianus Quintus*, that was hung as church-ship in a Copenhagen church not very many years since, and a large and perfectly finished model of the R.M.S.P. Company's steamship *Arcadian* that was last year dedicated as a church-ship at Saint James's Church, Bridge Road, Southampton. When one thinks of the many great names and events that might be commemorated by the hanging of appropriate ships in British churches and town-halls it seems certain that this revival of the old custom will be imitated elsewhere.

It can hardly have been without some hints drawn from the older church-ship of tradition that the first architectural models, examples of true shipbuilding in miniature, were made. As a theory it is attractive to suppose that such models may first have been made in the form of Mediterranean galleys. Crescentio's *Nautica Mediterranea* gives us, as well as the block-carved galeass of Lepanto, a galley that might well be copied from a built model, and it would be so impossible without actual timber construction to show the lightly built and complicated upperworks of a galley that the attempt might very naturally lead to building such a model from the keel upwards. In time it may be that research will throw more light upon the origins of ship-modelling elsewhere and enable us to see how and where it began, but when first we come across a record of it in England, in 1599, it is as no new thing. This earliest named model was described, by Phineas Pett, its maker, as having been "perfected, and exquisitely set out and rigged." In 1604 Phineas Pett built the *Disdain* for Prince Henry, a navigable ship-yacht so small that it was almost a large scale model, but in 1607 he made, mostly, as he says, with his own hands, a real model for the same prince, "most fairly garnished with carving and painting, and placed in a frame, arched, covered, and curtained with crimson tapestry." We could better spare such a mounting than the model it contained, but it at least shows that he knew his work to be worth the

28

best setting that he could devise. In 1634 Phineas Pett, grown too wise perhaps to sacrifice more of his own handiwork, had made, under his direction, a little ship for a still younger prince—Charles, then aged four—to disport himself withal, "who entertained it with a great deal of joy." This prince's plaything was mounted on a " carriage with wheels, resembling the sea," and it may be guessed that its dainty workmanship did not long outlive his first taking it in tow. It is interesting to note Phineas Pett's distinction between this " little ship " and his own "models"; the latter word, it is clear, was already appropriated to actual miniatures built from the plans of a proposed or existing ship. Mr. R. C. Anderson, *Mariner's Mirror*, Vol. X., p. 216, draws attention to an English scale-model brought to Sweden by its maker, Francis Sheldon, in 1658, and still preserved at Stockholm. Sheldon, a royalist refugee, gained the position of master-builder at Gothenburg in 1659, helped no doubt by this model, the oldest known English one of its class. His descendants were still in the Swedish service a century later. Pepys tells us, too, how Peter Pett kept up the model-making tradition of his family, and when blamed in 1667 for taking a boat to save his models of ships at the time of the Dutch raid, answered, " he did believe the Dutch would have made more advantage of the models than of the ships, and that the King had had a greater loss thereby."

Pepys mentions elsewhere his own pleasure in a model that he had hung up in his office for his instruction, and in time he acquired a collection of them that was less lucky than his library and, as such, has disappeared. As Duke of York, James II. had his collection, too, that was carefully kept in glass cases, as we learn from the *Travels* of Cosmo III., Grand Duke of Tuscany, 1669, where it is claimed that these models were of his own design. This too is scattered, but the Sergison collection, formed not much later and preserved until recently at Cuckfield, Sussex, is, though no longer in England, still fortunately intact. Model-making in England had the beginning of its literature, in Thomas Miller's *Complete Modellist*, as early as 1664, and the surviving specimens of 17th century English work at the craft show that something very near to perfection in it had then already been gained here.

If, as we have seen, rigged scale-models of actual ships were being made in England as early as the reign of Elizabeth, we can hardly suppose that they were peculiar to that country. King Christian IV. of Denmark is even said to have been himself a skilled modellist, and little as is yet known of them it becomes likely that by the end of the 16th century similar models were being made elsewhere in Europe. Such models, always of ships of war or of armed merchant ships, would, like Peter Pett's, be kept as precious State secrets until they became obsolete, and then either burnt as rubbish or given as playthings to high-born babes, so that it is not astonishing that records of them should be lacking.

In Holland the earliest models of this kind that survive date from the years between 1650 and 1670, and the Swedish *Amaranthe* model (Plate 22) is of the same date and class. The differences between Dutch, or Scandinavian, and English shipbuilding at this time were very marked, and even more different were the Dutch and English schools of model-making. The English model, however perfect, stops short when the work of the shipbuilder and the rigger are shown in her, much of her framing remains uncovered so that the vital parts of her construction can be seen, and lesser details, colouring, and sails are not given. The Dutch model, perhaps because of the presence then in Holland of so many church-ships to give the example, goes further, giving every detail of the ship when at sea, to her exact painting, even perhaps to her canvas, and if less useful as a guide to the shipbuilder concerned with construction, gives that much more to the artist who would know how such a ship looked when sailing. Sometimes, even, by removing the stern, the cabin may also be seen in every detail. This is not to say that no purely constructional models were then made out of England, of course, and some such still exist that date from the 17th century. The oldest surviving Danish model is, like most subsequent Danish naval models, of this class, and represents, unrigged and unfinished, the *Prins Carl*, of 1696.

In France, by 1678, and under the direction of Colbert's wonderful organizing genius, a system of model-making was established by which it was intended that the exact form and construction of a vessel of each of five rates should be perpetually fixed. Probably these models, none of which seems to have survived, were not completed with the carved work that would have distinguished any one particular ship of each rating, and as the form of the hull was especially to be perpetuated in them, it is likely that they were unrigged. The miniature vessels of all sorts that made the "flotilla of Versailles," although built on a reduced scale, were perhaps too large to be classed as models, for they seem to have had crews who

30

demonstrated in them the evolutions of fleets, thus bringing the sea to the King's doors.   Rigged models, however, can hardly have been a novelty in 1680, when Louis XIV. had a model of a first-rate ship "made, rigged and fitted out in all respects like the ship that was to be built after its pattern."   Though this ship no longer exists, the *Royal Louis* of 1692 (Plate 42) still survives to show how such a model might be finished; this is like the English models in being without sails, but in every other respect is complete down to the last detail of rigging and painting.   That the usual contemporary French ship-builder's model may have been left without painting and gilding as well as without sails, though entirely planked and fully rigged, is shown by the wreck of the once very beautiful model of *L'Agréable* of 1695 (Plate 45) decorated by Puget, whose designs for her carved work still exist.   In this the colouring is indicated by the use of different woods only, and the beautiful workmanship in what remains of the carving is nowhere concealed. Unfortunately this ship at some period of her history had been allowed to remain exposed to rain, with the result that her timbers had warped badly, making it difficult to restore her without a certain amount of re-building. Her mizen-mast down, her rigging in sad disorder, her guns gone, and despoiled of much of her carved work, I was permitted by the authorities at the Louvre to make some sketches of this model over twenty years ago, when she was removed from a lumber-room, along with the battered hulk of an old Dutch church-ship, here illustrated,

DUTCH CHURCH SHIP, *circa* 1670-1680. MUSÉE DE MARINE, PARIS

31

for that purpose. These two wrecks will perhaps be restored one day. They should both repay for reconstruction by competent hands, for no 17th-century ship-model could be undeserving of this, and while the Dutch ship, said to have been Napoleon's spoil of war, has such unusual features as a bench (*banc de quart*) fixed to the poop bulkhead, a defence with two portholes over the half-deck bulkhead, and a second row of cabin lights astern, L'*Agréable* is, both as a scale model and for its rare detail, of even greater interest.

With the coming of the 18th century we are no longer chronicling the beginnings of ship-modelling. Wherever ships were being built on the grand scale, there models of them were being made, and we still have examples in miniature of most classes of shipping that have sailed the seas since that time. At first it is rare to find any models of merchant ships, such as were built in private yards for private owners, but though it was not until the 19th century that these were much made except in Holland, we do find a few earlier examples. For models of obsolescent trading vessels of small size, even of ketches and schooners, to say nothing of more unusual types like our own Lancashire schooners, Humber keels and billy-boys, or Severn trows, we may look in vain in most modern museums; local types are better preserved in Holland than anywhere, perhaps, though this is excellently done in some other foreign museums, notably at Altona, but there are, at home as well as abroad, hundreds of traditional "folk-craft," so to call them, local traders or fishing-boats, that making a poor appearance, perhaps, beside the nobility of the sea in the form of ships of war, or even beside its plutocracy in the form of world traders, are yet of an interest to the student of ethnology, and of shipping in its widest sense, that should make it well worth while to preserve them in model form before it is too late. The professional seaman, whatever craft he sailed in, was given to making models of full-rigged ships rather than of any less dignified ship types, and the professional ship-modellist has always been kept busy in reproducing forms either experimental or in the forefront of the movement in contemporary naval architecture. We have now, however, in several countries, but especially in America, with its Ship Model Society, and in England, with its Society for Nautical Research, a large number of skilled amateur ship-modellists, many of them artists, who are all very much alive to the interest of bygone shipping, and although, naturally enough, these are largely fascinated by the possibilities of

32

reconstructing from existing contemporary data the most picturesque and imposing ships of past centuries, some amongst them are taking up this other no less attractive subject of obsolete or obsolescent local types. In such ways, with an increasing number of ship-modellists and diggers out of buried facts, the world may one day have what it is at present far from having—at least one great marine museum where all the efforts made by man towards expressing himself in terms of shipbuilding might be arranged in model form as in a family-tree. If the principle of such an arrangement were adopted even in a comparatively small existing collection, the gaps would become very obvious as one worked backwards in time, while in the largest collection we should find that, taking warships alone, while the past two centuries were over-represented enormously, in earlier periods whole centuries would follow one another with blank after blank; and though the whole wide world might be more or less represented by a number of " folk-craft "—junks, canoes, and catamarans of all kinds—hundreds of equally interesting local types of the home coast would certainly be missing. It is in filling up such gaps with models to represent all that travel and investigation can discover that amateur ship-modellists will render Science their greatest service.

VOTIVE SHIP AT VENICE. JAL, 1835

THE DEVELOPMENT OF SQUARE-RIGGED SHIPS.

NO genealogical-tree of ships that could yet be put together would be of that irrefutable kind demanded by heralds or lawyers; and although much work has been spent on the evidence, all efforts at tracing their first parents must as yet be considered as tentative. We are offered one tempting Father Adam to the whole shipping race that is not quite as lightly to be dismissed from that place as *Noah's Ark*, the former favourite. This is the sailing ship of ancient Egypt. It is beyond dispute that most of the arts and activities of civilised man had their first beginning in Egypt, and that in the earlier ages, as far as is yet known, ships were brought to a higher state of perfection in that country than in any other contemporary state. It would be difficult to prove beyond the possibility of doubt, however, that the ideas of making a boat, paddles, rudder, or sails, went, either separately or together, out from Egypt all over the world. One primitive form of boat, that of wicker covered with hide, would seem likely to have originated amongst people living in a champaign country, where the hunting of large beasts was varied with fishing, and where timber was scarce; yet the ribs of the framework of a modern ship may quite reasonably be traced back to the withies of a coracle. Another primitive form of boat, the hollowed log, must, one would think, have originated in a land of great trees, such as Egypt never had; and yet this log is the keel of the same framework. The Egyptian ship, evolved, as has clearly been shown, from a keel-less, rib-less, reed-bundle raft, even as a sea-going vessel had neither ribs nor keel, and in its shape still held the contour of the original reed-bundle—the bowl of an elongated spoon with ends raised and brought to a point would come very near to it—while its stout planks, though now firmly fixed edge to edge, still imitated in wood the arrangement of the parallel bundles of reeds that were lashed together to make the raft. It seems certain, then, that the dug-out, with the straighter lines that were dictated by its material, has had its influence in producing the straight-keeled ship of the modern world, even if we deny that coracles have had any influence in suggesting its ribbed frame.

34

Coracles are sufficiently wide-spread, but to enumerate the countries where dug-out canoes are used would be to cover almost all the world, for as cheap and serviceable small craft they survive long after the more difficult art of ship-building is acquired. A good instance of this was the white-painted dug-out that I remember seeing years ago carried as a dinghey aboard a barque from the port of Gefle in Sweden, but the same primitive boat makes a punt for Red Sea dhows, and shows a persistence elsewhere that is in itself perhaps due to a momentum acquired in its very long career.

There are two ways of increasing the value of a dug-out. Its want of stability may be corrected by lashing two together or by adding a dummy boat—an outrigger; but although almost the whole interest of Pacific Island craft centres round the varieties of these, we can leave them out of account in treating of the origins of European shipping, and here the second way, that of increasing its capacity by raising planks upon its sides, becomes most important.

We have, preserved for us by long burial in bog, some actual prehistoric North European dug-outs with plank-heightened sides, and Scandinavian rock-carvings of the Early Bronze Age, as far as they can be trusted, seem to give us a type of war-canoe that is remarkably like that of Uganda. Here the log, hollowed out and raised by a plank along the sides, is prolonged forward into a ram beak at the water-line, while the side-planks are joined at each end to an upright " stem," morticed into the log. The fact that the Uganda boat, so like in other things, is also paddled like the pre-historic Scandinavian one, and even has its bow " stem " adorned with a similar beast's head with horns—the same horns-talisman that 17th-century " Wild Irishmen " bore as an ox-skull on the bows of their sailing curaghs, and that in the modified form of a shark's-tail is carried by sailing-ships of to-day at their bowsprit-ends—seems to imply that somehow these two, though so widely separated, derive from a common source, and one that, as far as we can tell, was not Egyptian.

To this source, whatever it may have been, may most naturally be traced the ram beak, most familiar to us in the Greek or Roman galley, but coming to them through Phoenicia from Asia, for this is clearly the pointed end of an original log canoe, still remaining at the water-line, though the log has become a keel, and the single plank has become a whole series of rib-supported planks one over another. Boats from grave mounds in Norway and from Nydam

35

Bog show that development there followed the same line—the dug-out became first a wide, slightly hollowed keel-piece, then a true keel, only hollowed a little right forward where it rose towards the stem, and sometimes given a spur or ram beak just below the water-line, the "skeg" or beard, the name of which is still kept in very similar senses—in English, of a projection at the stern; in Dutch, *schegge*, of one at the bow; in Danish, *skaegget*, of the beak itself. This "skeg" soon ceased to be a ram, however, and the Norse "long-ship," in spite of its oars and its single square sail, was very unlike a Greek or Roman galley; even more different was a Norse round-ship or trader from a Greek or Roman merchant-ship.

These are differences that remained characteristic of Northern and Mediterranean ships for century after century and are not yet entirely obliterated in small craft, so it is worth while to enumerate them, comparing a Roman merchant ship of the second century

NORTHERN AND ROMAN MERCHANTMEN

A.D. with a Norse trading ship of the tenth. Firstly, the methods of construction were quite different. The Roman ship's stem and stern-post seem to have been covered right up to the forward edge with its planking; the Northern stem and stern-post stood well out. Even more striking, the Roman ship was carvel-built, with planks edge to edge as in the rib-less Egyptian ship and in modern wooden vessels; the Northern ship was clinker-built, with planks that overlapped one another, a method mostly reserved for quite small boats to-day. Used as we are to seeing these building methods alongside of one another, we hardly perhaps realise what an ocean of difference there is between them historically. It is probable, too, that, as in modern ships, the frame of a Roman ship was built before

36

being planked over, while the ribs and beams would be put into a Northern ship after the planking was finished and fastened, a survival of which is found in 17th- century Dutch ship-building, where several planks were raised on the keel and " stems "—an under-boat being formed, in fact—before any ribs were put in place. The curves made by the sheer were as different; the Northern ship rising almost if not quite equally fore and aft, while the Roman merchant ship, as here illustrated, rose far more suddenly astern, repeating the rush-bundle outline of the Egyptian ship from whence she probably derived it. The two rudders, contrasting with the Northern single one, and the projecting beam-ends along her sides came also, it seems likely, from Egypt, where both are found, and the mast, with its masthead block or *calcet* of hardwood for the ties, the square sail with several lifts to the two-spar yard, and the cabin aft may all derive from the same source. The shrouds seen in the Roman ship are new since Ancient Egypt, where they were backstays rather than shrouds, but these, although common to both, have their "eyes" *below* the *calcet* in the Roman ship, and *above* the hounds that serve the same purpose in the Northern one. The Roman sail has a similar square shape, but in all else is quite unlike the Northern one. The latter has (probably) reefs, and a vargord or bowlines; but its yard is without lifts, and comes down when it is taken in, in these things like the North Norwegian fishing boats of the present day that carry on nearly all of the old Norse traditions of build and rig. The Roman sail is without reefs and without bowlines, while its yard in ordinary weather stays aloft, the sail being brailed up to it with many lines that run from the foot of the sail, up through rings sewn to its seams, to the yard, and thence down, either straight, or in some cases by way of the other side of the sail, to the deck. When these lines are partially hauled on, the sail is diminished, on one side or on both, much as by reefing; when they are hauled right home it is brailed close up, and is then furled by sailors who go out along the yard on a foot-rope— a thing lost for centuries but re-invented when reefing was introduced for topsails in 17th-century ships. The Northern sail is not a mere simplification of this complicated gear, even if, possibly through the leathern sails of the ships of the Venetian-British fleets, it may ultimately derive from the same source; besides this the Roman sail is not solitary, for on a bowsprit-like foremast a little foresail, practically a spritsail, is carried, and above the mainsail are set lower

37

and upper "raffee" topsails. On the whole one gets from the Roman vessel an impression of complexity, the result of age-long development and many contacts, and from the Northern vessel one of fresh simplicity that suggests quick growth from a single source.

These two types, Southern and Northern, although belonging to different periods, were good examples for comparison because both were square sailed: had we taken a contemporary Southern ship to compare with our Northern one, the sails, even, would have been of a different shape, for the lateen, or lateen-lug, had then already displaced the square sail, except, perhaps, as a storm-sail, and had brought its own particular gear. No longer bearing the classical Greek or Roman stamp in details, the Southern ship had yet changed little in contour, and the foremast still raked over the bows, the steering was still done with the Latin side-rudders, the yard was still a two-spar one, beam-ends still projected along the sides, the ties of the yard ran through a *calcet* at the mast-head and the eyes of the shrouds encircled the mast beneath it. Such ships seem commonly to have been two-masters, but we find them pictured sometimes with three masts and sometimes with one.

Passing over the changes that have taken place in both Southern and Northern ships during the years between, but have left them both true to type, let us take for a second contrast the one-masted Southerner of the sculptured shrine of St. Peter Martyr at Pisa and a typical Northerner of the same date, *circa* 1340, an interesting time

NORTHERN AND SOUTHERN SHIPS, *circa* 1340

because it just precedes the blending of both types in the carrack, and the practical uniformity of square-rig for all Europe that was a speedy result.

38

Both ships have acquired " castles," fore, after, and top; but these are as unlike as their different origins would lead one to expect. The Southern after-castle is but a modification of the Roman poop, and is really not unlike the poop of the terra-cotta ship from Amathus, of the 6th century B.C., while the fore-castle, though Roman ships often had a fore-gallery, is, in the South, a new and rather unusual feature. The top-castle is deep and narrow, and although it is not placed as a " half-top " altogether abaft the mast-head *calcet*, as was the more general plan in Mediterranean lateeners throughout the Middle Ages and down to the last days of the galley, its larger part is aft. The eyes of the rigging come beneath this top, and from it a Jacob's-ladder leads to the deck, the shrouds, set up with blocks, being without ratlines. The yard, a two-spar one, is controlled by ties, that lead through a *calcet*, by a parrel, and at its extremities by *ostes* (vangs) and *orses*, that hold its fore-end down, serving somewhat as the mizen-bowlines on a 17th-century ship's lateen-mizen. It is worth while to notice these peculiarities not only because they always remained typical of the lateen-rigged galley, but because we shall find some of them again in the 15th-century carrack. This Pisa ship shows the Latin side-rudder with its gear, in relief and in fullest detail, putting the projecting beam-ends and retreating stem and stern post beyond doubt in the same way, and in spite of some omissions is, on the whole, the best example of a Mediterranean ship of this period.

The English ship, founded on those in a manuscript at the Bodleian Library, and confirmed by contemporary seals, shows how the separation of types persists—the equal sheer fore and aft is still there, though castles now crown both ends of the ship, and the cutting away of the stern-post to allow of a tiller working over it has brought the after-castle lower than it was when the side-rudder was still used. The clinker-built hull, with projecting stem and stern-post, disguised, perhaps, under stripes of colour that follow the strakes, is defended by leaf-shaped fender-cleats nailed on to the planking. The shrouds have ratlines, and are probably set up to rings or hearts, invisible inboard. The sail is still square, but has reefs evenly distributed from top to bottom; it still has no lifts, but its bowlines, the ship itself being now too short for them, are set up to a bowsprit that is given a serrated " bowsprit-comb " beneath, to which the bowlines are adjusted according to the wind. This bow-sprit serves as yet no other purpose. The stay is set up around the stem, a vacant space being left in the planking there that serves for this purpose and for the cable as well—the "hawse," or neck, of the ship. Another thing that an earlier, or even a contemporary, ship might have shown would be the Northern "half-top" type of

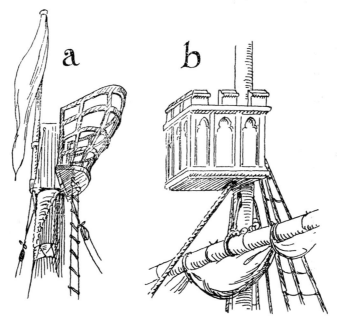

A. HALF-TOP OF 18th-CENTURY GALLEY, LATIN STYLE
B HALF-TOP OF 14th CENTURY NORTHERN SHIP

top-castle which is exactly the opposite of the Mediterranean half-top, the hounds for the tie being set in the mast below it, not in a *calcet* above, and the rigging rising above its crosstrees, not below them, while the whole is before, not abaft, the mast. These contrarieties, except that the top is round and encircles the whole masthead, still exist here, though less evident.

Roughly we may call these two 14th-century ships the father and mother of the 15th-century carrack; now let us look at their offspring.

It will be convenient to take a full-blown carrack that has acquired fore and mizen masts; for one thing because there is conflicting evidence as to which of these masts was first added, although they were seldom both present before the middle of the 15th century, and a one-masted carrack was before either. We are still sadly ignorant of the details of ships before 1400, and hardly know how to reconcile the very varying and often unconvincing

40

pictures of them with written records, or to distinguish one sort of ship from another. We are able to see gradual changes in the shape of "castles," to trace the development of the rudder, and to discover something of the ancient reefing methods, but it is difficult to get much further. Names refer only to differences of build or size, for all had the single square sail in the North, and yet are known by different names, as ships, cogs, barges, balingers, etc., and some ship-names used in the North were given in the Mediterranean to vessels that can have had little but tonnage in common with them; but we do know what a carrack of the middle of the 15th century was like, better perhaps than we know the appearance of a carrack of a century later, and we find that this, though it originated in the Mediterranean as an imitation to some extent of Northern ships, was practically the same thing in all parts of Europe. We have some excellent Italian and French examples that agree, at all events, very closely with the wonderfully detailed Flemish *kraeck* of the engraver who signs his work ⚓. (*see p.* 42), giving only slightly less complete renderings of the detail of the rigging, and sometimes adding that of the sails, furled in the Flemish engraving, or of the decks, there hidden.

Great depth was the chief distinction as to build between the 15th-century carrack and other square-rigged sailing ships of her time, for certain of her Southern features had already extended to other types of Northern ship. The fuller bows and much rounder stern, the carvel planking, with its protecting upright skids and lengthwise wales, serving the purpose of the cleats on the clinker-built ship of 1340 in defending it against hoisted weights or wharfside friction, and the greater development of the "castles," are all striking when compared with their counterparts in this earlier ship. Not only are the castles themselves more nearly a part of the ship herself than they were, but they are given, still higher, fighting-platforms that stand above them much as the earliest "castles" or "stages" stood above the deck, and these have tilt-frames over them upon which awnings, or in battle, nettings, can be stretched. Under the forecastle a noble archway leads to the bitts and to the great, staring, round hawses, beneath which would probably be a trough, the "manger," to catch the water that is drawn in with the cable, or bursts in at them, in spite of the "bucklers" that Carpaccio's Genoese carrack in *St. Ursula's Arrival at Cologne* shows us, allowing it to run back through scuppers into

41

THE KRAECK OF ⦙⦙, *circa* 1450

the sea. Along the waist are "cowbridges," gangways of thwart-ships-laid planking that rise, forward, to meet the forecastle, this raised end, with the arch, making the "cowbridge-head." Similar "cowbridges" or "corridors" run along at each side abaft the main-mast, too, sometimes rising aft to meet the castle at the poop, sometimes coming together to make a complete deck for a few plank's breadth abaft the mast, and showing how the half-deck, like the upper deck amidships, originated as two separate gangways, joined later by a grating and eventually made one deck.

Sometimes Mediterranean carracks are drawn with the projecting beam-ends along the sides that, as we have seen, were a feature of Egyptian vessels, and originated probably in the projecting thwart-ends of some primitive craft in which these, as they often are in such canoes, were lashed to a gunwale. This Southern feature is not a constant one in all carracks, but their rig is invariably Southern in type. The shrouds are without ratlines in so many carrack pictures that the few in which they are represented may be considered as the mistakes of Northern artists; a Jacob's ladder abaft the mast takes their place on the main-mast only. The eyes of the shrouds make a sort of woolding below the trestle-trees of the top, and they are set up, below, sometimes with Southern-style blocks, sometimes with Northern-style heart-shaped dead-eyes, sometimes with both, dead-eyes being given only to a few aftermost shrouds, and these may be either inside the bulwarks, in Southern style, or on modern looking channels outside, as in " W A ' s " print.

The sails are main, fore, and mizen, with a tiny main-topsail, that is rarely shown set and was at first entirely a "top" sail, braced down to the top and sheeted to the top-rim, not to the yard-arms; to these a spritsail was not added until near the century's end. The mizen is a lateen, its yard in Southern carracks still given the galley-fashion *mouton*, a rope attached to its lower end, by which it was drawn back and changed over from side to side, as required, by being up-ended *before* the mast, but in " W A's " *kraeck* the mizen yard is already given a ship-style lift at its upper end, that is in principle exactly the same as those of Elizabethan ships, and changes the mizen *abaft* the mast. These opposite ways of "changing" a lateen yard cause an opposite placing of the "half-top" above it in a 16th-century square-rigged ship to that in a contemporary galley. So that the upper end of the yard shall meet with no obstruction in changing, the former has its half-top *before* the mast, the latter *abaft*

43

it. The carrack usually has no mizen-top, nor half-top even, "W⋏'s" being almost alone in this. At first sight the latter might appear to have galley-fashion *ostes* with its ship-fashion lift; the former are actually two sheets, though, led as far astern as they can go until the "outligger," not yet in fashion, comes in to spread the single sheet further aft.

Lifts were not used on the main yard of the English ship of 1340—as we have seen, they were foreign to the North; here on the carrack, with their two lower blocks, they are much in evidence, as are also the "martnetts"—ropes branching like a cat-o'-nine-tails, French *martinet*—that gather in the upper corners of the sail in furling it. More tackles, going from blocks at the foot of the sail to others below the yard, and not shown by " W⋏," gather it up into a huge bagful of wind, awkward one would think to handle, especially as the men lay "overthwart the sail-yard" to furl it, without footropes, which had been left behind with the old Roman square sail. Bagginess was a quality desired, though, the sail being given overlapping seams or stitched to bolt-ropes shorter than the cloths in order to gain it, and a middle line of gathering was made as well, that divided the sail into two great wind-bags, or with the two smaller ones of the deep bonnet, laced on to increase its size below, four in all. No wonder that in saying of Sathanas' tail that it was "broader than of a carrike is the sayl," Chaucer should have thought that he had amply stated the matter. A "bowge" drew this great sail in towards the mast by its middle, and bowlines stiffened its weather-leech, but though its braces had pendants its sheets were still single ropes, as in the older Northern ship. Its canvas was for greater strength made "double," that is, with one set of cloths crossing another at right angles, though bonnets might be "single," and lateen mizens were always so. These crossed seams are always conspicuous in carrack pictures of the time. The fashion of "doubling" each cloth by folding it down the middle of its length before seaming was prevalent in the next century, as Crescentio tells us.

It has seemed worth while, even in a brief account of ship-evolution, to describe the 15th-century carrack at some length, not only because in it are combined features that belong to two distinct schools of ship-building and rigging, both of which are represented by models in this book, but also because we find in it the origins of many of the features of later ships. "Carrack," as a name,

44

CARRACK *circa* 1550, AFTER BRUEGEL

45

was still retained down to the end of the 18th century, especially for great armed cargo ships used by the Spanish and Portuguese, but denoted then no difference in rig.

In developing, the three-masted-ship rig, that seems to have begun with the carrack, by the 16th century had grown in some ways less Southern. The shrouds were now always set up with heart-shaped dead-eyes, the chains of which came over the outside edge of the channels, not through holes in them as in " W⋔ 's," and were given ratlines, leaving henceforth to galleys only the old Jacob's ladder. The mizen-lift got the better of the *mouton*, though that galley-style gear remained in use for some time, especially when a second, "bonaventure," mizen was added. Pieter Bruegel, one of whose ships is here shown (*p. 45*), gives mizens of both types. With anything but the smallest of topmasts set before them it was impossible to make the two sheaves of a galley-style *calcet* serve for the ties, and after the middle of the century a thwartships "ass-head" or "moor's-head" cap, over which the ties ran at each side of the topmast, seems to have replaced it on all but English ships. In these latter the old Northern hounds were doubled, so that the ties ran through them below the top, and the cap, made rectangular, with a hole through which the topmast passed, avoiding the need for a lashing, was fitted alongships, a fashion that later, when ties and halyards were replaced by jears, became universal. (See later illustration, *a, b, c.*) With these new fittings topmasts could easily be struck, and were at once, with their sails, made higher. The hull of the early 16th-century ship or carrack retained the 15th-century shape below except that the round stern in its first years gave place to a square tuck and gun-ports were cut in the sides; above, the "castles" grew more consolidated, and the "stern-castle," narrowing aloft, projected aft with counter over counter, overhanging the rudder considerably. Its sail plan had altered as a result of decreasing the mainsail in size and greatly increasing the foresail, and not only were topsails made much bigger, and given to fore, main, and, as lateens, even to mizen masts, but top-gallant-sails were sometimes added above them, even studding-sails of some sort were in use, and a spritsail was set flying on the bowsprit. This spar, set to starboard of the stem-head all through the 16th-century, and for still longer on English ships, kept its old uses as a means of setting up the bowlines, and as a place for the boarding-grapnel and its chain, which on the Danish *Norse Lion*, of the mid-17th century, Plate 19, is still to be seen there. Almost

46

balancing the bowsprit, an "outligger" for the mizen sheet was added astern. From fairly early in the century a boomkin, the French *chique*, was often run out beneath the projecting forecastle, to which the foretacks were led; with the coming of a lower beak-head this spar was gradually abandoned, the tacks being led to a comb-cleat beneath it, instead.

During the reign of Henry VIII., England, like other countries at the same time, began to experiment with new types of war vessels that might combine the advantages of oared galleys with those of sailing ships; one of these, the galleon, permanently influenced the form of subsequent armed vessels, to which this name was given, especially by the Spanish, who still had Vera Cruz "galleons" in the 18th century. Built longer, and discarding to some extent the towering "castles" that were ceasing to be of much advantage since improved artillery had lengthened the range of fire, these ships had instead of the projecting forecastle of the mediaeval ship a straight fighting beak, the origin of the curved, ornamental beak of later days with its figure head, still called by names equivalent to "galleon" or "galleon figure" in most North European languages. This beak was at first a metal-tipped ram, given either to high-stemmed bows that rose curving in above it like those of a Flemish hulk, or else added below an old-fashioned projecting forecastle as in Furttenbach's model, but gradually a new type of bow gained ground that stopped short at the level of the beak, the forward part of the shortened forecastle being given a beakhead-bulkhead that corresponded to the cowbridge-head at its after part, and the beak itself repeating the under framing alone of the old forecastle. The fore mast, always stepped rather far forward, was now placed before the beakhead-bulkhead, this change resulting in what is perhaps the most characteristic feature of the galleon or ship of the end of the 16th century, and the bowsprit was stepped to starboard both of it and of the stem-head.

Another contemporary feature, trivial but almost as characteristic, is the very general use of crowfoot attachments. We already saw the beginning of these in the mizen-lifts and martnetts of W⚓ and Bruegel, but in a ship of near 1600 we have usually a greater complication of them in both mizen-lifts and martnetts, and added to these we have more on the stays, which, carrying as yet no sails, are made use of for the attachment of braces, bowlines, and the standing parts of halyards, even. The object of a crowfoot is, of course, to spread the strain of a pull over a greater length of rope or spar, and it is still used on the sides of awnings and boat-

CROWFOOT ATTACHMENTS IN A "SHIP ROYAL" OF 1600

covers with a similar purpose. The old riggers seem to have taken great delight in the quaint patterns that they make, for in a "ship royal" they are added beyond what was found useful or necessary in lesser ships, and their names in other languages, meaning "cock's foot," "spider," "goose-foot," give similar expression to this fondness.

The sails of such a ship, though not positive "wind-bags," are still made to bag a good deal; the practice over a century later, even, was to cut the sails the same length as the yard, enough being taken in by the sailmaker in stitching them to the bolt-rope to leave the yard-arms clear of the earings. The theory was that the wind should be held in the sail, and not allowed to escape too quickly at the lee leech. This certainly gave these older ships the *appearance* of making the fullest use of the wind, and in going free these baggy sails may have been as profitable as they were picturesque, even though they might, in sailing on a wind, prove spendthrifts of all such gains. A shallow bonnet, and sometimes a similar sail below that, the "drabler," was laced on at the bottom of the sail much as in the 15th-century carrack; the method of lacing it with eyelet-holes and loops, called "latchets," being exactly that still used for fastening together the wall-cloths of marquees or in those leggings still worn in the country, that lace up in front with eyelets and latchets of the ancient sort. To lace or unlace a bonnet it was necessary to get hold of the sail first, from below, and "lee-fangs," made fast to cringles at the foot of the sail, were used to draw it within reach.

A spritsail, the yard of which ran up and down on a "horse" beneath the bowsprit, stowing alongside the beakhead when furled, was the rule until about the end of the century, when, the "horse" abolished, the spritsail-yard became more permanently fixed out on the bowsprit, with a spritsail-topsail added on a little mast of its own at the bowsprit-end, though this at first only in very great ships. The main-bowlines still, as in 1340 and earlier, led out on the bowsprit, and its use as a place for the boarding-grapnel was not quite abandoned; often, however, a couple of sharp shear-hooks were fitted at the bowsprit-end to match those of the lower yard-arms, and aid in cutting an enemy's rigging.

One of the marked features of the ships of the South had been their galleries astern. " W⚓ " shows us how a gallery was added abaft the carrack's cabin, but although a stern-gallery is not very uncommon in the middle quarters of the 16th century, it is not until the last quarter that we find it, with quarter-galleries added, in all larger ships, and doubled, as an upper and lower gallery, in "ships royal." At first quite open above, we later find that curved timbers, or sometimes irons, connected its rim with the side of the ship, helping the brackets beneath in the task of supporting it, but serving also as a frame over which an awning could be spread. Just as what were tilt-frames, nettings, and awnings in the carrack developed later into solid structures, so this temporary roof over the gallery led to the making of close-galleries with a permanent roof and a row of glazed lights above what had been the rim level of the old open gallery. Though Monson commends the open quarter-gallery as giving a quick means of giving commands from the cabin to men on deck, its invitation of incendiary missiles was its fatal drawback. At the corners of the open galleries of great ships, and also at prominent parts of these ships themselves, especially at the

49

top of the poop, it was the custom to fix little turrets. A good instance of this is the *Ark Royal*, a picture of which vessel has been used as a base for models of the *Great Harry*. These were the days of Nonsuch House, and freakish architecture was enjoyed for its own sake, but some at least of these turrets seem also to have been used as lanterns. The church-ship from the Mariakirke at Bergen, Plate 14, even has turret guns pointing from them, but this is an anticipation of modern armament that can hardly be taken seriously, and may even be part of the " restoration " from which she has suffered.

The form of these galleries and of their turrets was at first varied with each ship rather than according to its nationality, but as the 17th century wore on, each school of marine architecture settled down into its own peculiar style, for galleries as for beakheads, consoles, port-wreaths, and the rest, and it is easy to distinguish between a Dutch, a French, or an English ship by these alone. As compared with the late 16th-century ship, the mid-17th-century one looked, astern, more compact and at the same time broader, simply as a result of this closing in of the galleries; the closing of the after gallery especially covered up the hollow second counter that had been so noticeable in the older stern, and the carving, that in the older ship had been a comparatively slight touch of decoration, doing little more than lighten the constructive features by removing a little superfluous wood, given a greater continuous surface upon which to expand blossomed forth in rich relief. A large space on the upper part of the stern was generally kept sacred to the painted or carved name-emblem of the ship, a custom that started in the 16th century. This panel was called in Dutch, *tafereel*, " picture," whence the English word " taferel," and in French, *tutèle*, or *dieu conduit*, from the old custom of naming ships after saints, which so often caused a tutelary image to be put there. At the top of this panel the poop was crowned by a piece of carving that held the cranks of the poop-lanterns, often representing a pair of sea-lions, angels, or cupids, as supporters to a central shield or boss; and a pair of carved figures, called in Dutch *hoekmannen*, " corner men," and cut on a larger scale than the other carvings, were fixed to the angles above the quarter-galleries at either side of it. Below came the stern windows, and then the old rim of the gallery, called by the Dutch *slingerlijst*, and by them made curved like Cupid's bow. Beneath what had been the gallery was a hollow counter with a

50

tiller-hole and under this in Dutch and other foreign ships a square-tuck stern with its portholes.

As compared with the Dutch stern (c) the English one (d), suiting its build, remained much more reticently carved, the lines of

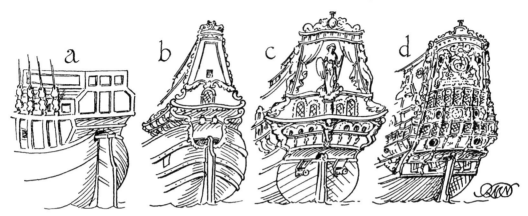

STERNS: ROUND, SQUARE-TUCK, AND ENGLISH 17th-CENTURY STYLE

construction, themselves much straighter, were made to divide most of the surface into small panels, glazed where light was needed, carved or painted elsewhere, and continued down below the stern portholes. With this lighter style of carving the quarter-pieces and quarter-galleries were, of course, correspondingly light. But the upper part of the poop, though smaller in detail and more compact, was not so very unlike that of a Dutch ship: it is below the counter that the English stern is most different, for while the Dutch one still has the square-tucked *spiegel*, "looking-glass," shape of the 16th century, the English one is made to round up to a transom below the counter somewhat as it did in the *kraeck* of W꜀꜆, but with the difference that the planking of this "round-tuck" was not, as there and as in the round-sterned Dutch ship of Memlinc (a) or its descendant flight or *fluitschip* (b), brought round and full to the stern-post as well. This new stern, of course, gave a much cleaner run and improved the ship's sailing qualities, but, like the English capstan, pump, cap, etc., it was not for some time imitated by continental builders, amongst whom the French seem to have been the first to see its merits, and there are still vessels of some size in which the 16th-century square tuck, and even the 15th-century round stern, survive, though these are but of local occurrence.

In French shipbuilding foreign influence was felt in turn from Holland and England, and no very definite national style seems to

51

have been adopted until after the Dutch and English styles were well-established, and with ship-decoration it was the same. When, under the influence of Colbert, the best available native talent was secured for ship-building, this soon resulted also in a French school of ship-carving, of which Toulon was the chief seat. Influenced partly, no doubt, by galley-carving, which gave great scope for figure-work in relief, and partly by the fact that Puget, "the French Michael Angelo," was a leading spirit in this school, the decoration of a French stern was made to depart a great deal from traditional forms, and sculptors and practical-minded naval architects were often at variance. The whole was treated as freely as contemporary land architecture would have allowed, the shapes and positions of stern windows being greatly varied; *bouteilles* resembling half-lanterns were substituted for galleries on the quarters, and a wealth of florid design, with much undercutting and a free use of large mythological figures, was lavished upon every part.

Differences as great existed in the carved work of the beak-head and of the top-sides generally of the ships of these three nations, and besides this their whole build was usually enough to distinguish them at sight. The Dutch, having shallow water round their coasts, built their vessels with floors very nearly flat, while French and English vessels were sharper and deeper. Two things especially one notices in Dutch-built ships; one is that they have clinker-built "cage-work" and bulkheads, a legacy probably from ships such as Memlinc painted on the St. Ursula casket at Bruges (a), where the same clinker-planked "cage-work" is present, another is the very generous supply of fender-bolts with which their comparatively slight timbers are studded, but the spacing of wales, and the positions of decks and channels are just as characteristic. It has already been seen that Dutch and other Northern ship-building started in the opposite way to English, French, or Southern building— the planking being started before fitting the ribs; this contrariness went further, for English ships when built were launched stern-first, and Dutch bow-first. The Dutch and Northern builders also launched a ship before completing her upperworks, adding her beak, or building up her stern, while English and Southern practice was to launch a ship completed to the last bit of carving.

In rig, while little national peculiarities existed here and there, as in the matter of caps and lift and sheet blocks, the sail-plan was everywhere much the same; any new thing being so rapidly copied

52

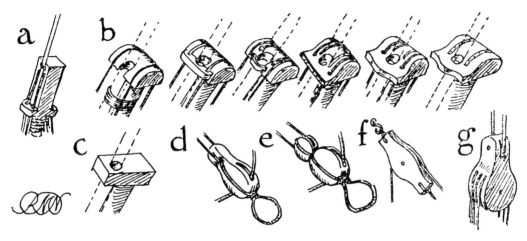

a. CALCET   b. DUTCH AND FRENCH CAPS IN DEVELOPMENT, 16th TO 18th CENTURY
c. ENGLISH CAP   d. CONTINENTAL TOPSAIL-SHEET BLOCK   e. ENGLISH DITTO
f. DUTCH LIFT BLOCK   g. RAM-HEAD BLOCK FOR TIES OF LOWER YARD

that it is usually difficult to know which country should have the credit of its invention. The early years of the 17th century brought the spritsail-topsail into general use, its advantages having been proved on the "ships royal" to which it was first given. Following close on this came the square mizen-topsail, a handier sail than the old lateen one, which is only found on the largest ships, and there is so seldom shown set that it seems unlikely to have been much used. As with most new things in the way of sails, this square mizen-topsail was given first only to very large ships. A square sail called a "crossjack" seems to have been used occasionally as a storm trysail on the mizen and to have given its name to the cro'jack yard, the *vergue sèche*, "bare yard," of the French, to which this topsail was extended below. At first this new sail seems to have been added even when two mizen-masts were carried, as, for instance, in pictures of the English *Prince Royal* of 1610, and probably, though its lateen yard, like the spritsail-yard, is missing, in the Flemish ship at Madrid, Plates 9 and 10; but the bonaventure-mizen soon disappeared, probably helped out of existence by this new sail. This produced a fresh balance in the sail-plan—topsails, whose yards were then still only half the length of lower yards, began to grow squarer, topgallantsails became a more every-day part of every big ship's suit of sails, and the spritsail-topsail was made somewhat bigger. The common 17th-century rig is, in fact, just the common 16th-century rig with the addition of a square sail to top

53

off each extremity, one over the spritsail, one over each topsail, and another over the lateen mizen. This was not, of course, just so much extra canvas, for with these higher sails came a reduction in relative size of the others, and especially of the courses. With this readjustment came the addition of backstays to help the shrouds. Soon after the middle of the century two other innovations were made; one, the introduction of reefing—at first by one band of reefs at the head of the topsail, to be followed towards the end of the century by a second, and another, that still more altered the appearance of the ship, the addition of triangular stay-sails like those already in long use on hoys (see Plate 69). The latter were probably looked upon as superfluities at first, and are rarely put into models or pictures. Running on light stays of their own, beneath main and mizen, and fore and main topmast, stays, they did not disturb the old use of stays as attachments for braces and bowlines. The use of stays as attachments for halyards had by this time been given up, and the old crowfoot fittings were now found only for the spritsail-topmast-backstay, or "craneline," that was set up to the fore-stay, for the mizen-topmast-stay that was led branching to the aftermost shroud of the main-rigging, and for the mizen-lift. Towards the end of the century jears replaced the old ties of the lower yards and their lifts, instead of coming in under the top, were led up to the cap.

The beak, all through the 17th century, was growing shorter, thicker, and more recurved, the fore tacks were, towards 1650, led through holes bored in this instead of through a "comb" beneath it, and later they were led through blocks at the same place. Down to this beak the bowsprit, stepped amidships, even in English ships, by the middle of the century, was still very firmly gammoned; for only at the very end of the century do we find a bobstay to give it any additional support, in spite of the fact that the strain of all the other masts comes eventually, by means of stays, upon the bowsprit. Bowsprit-shrouds of the modern kind were still far away, though a sort of "shrouds of the bowsprit"—a gammoning with dead-eyes and ratlines—was for a short time fitted in English ships, as *e.g.*, in the *Soveraigne of the Seas*, Plates 17 and 18.

During the 17th century much exchange of ideas had been going on between the great shipbuilding nations, and by the coming of the 18th, although in ships there was still diversity enough as to their decoration and build, they were fast growing more alike.

54

French and Spanish builders had arrived at their own compromises between Dutch and English extremes, and the former especially were giving so much attention to the theory and practice of ship-building that they were already beginning to take up the position that they held during most of the century, as the first ship-designers of the world.

In English ships there had always been a wholesome tendency to decorate the construction rather than to construct decoration, and this was carried to a fine point in the years about 1700. The conventional lion had for at least a century been everywhere the favourite figure-head, and it is interesting to see how it is adapted by ship-carvers to the changing beak. The Englishman's lion is now great of head, with a fine full-bottomed wig, his forelegs are bent back at a racking angle and his ribs are extraordinarily prominent, but he fits the curve of the ship's head absolutely, and the same thing happens if a man on horseback is carved there instead. On the magnificent Cuckfield *St. George*, we even find the saint and the dragon brought as beautifully into the right form by making the dragon bend his back into the desired curve. Astern it is the same; though, borrowed from the French, we find an open gallery re-introduced in another form, the poop is outlined with the simplest of curved masses, set out by the ship-builder, and the carved work, however bold, is adapted perfectly to these. Such a rounded poop, resplendent with its bright yellow or gold, must have had an effect like that of a wind-cropped furze-bush in full bloom. This simplification of mass in ship-carving was gained also by the Dutch and the Spanish, each in their own way, but French ship-decorators, and the Danes, deserting the Dutch style in imitation of them, continued much longer to construct decoration astern for the sake of its imposing effect. When we remember that galleys, with their flyaway caryatides and florid sculptures in general, were still in vogue in fashion-making France, we see why through much of the 18th century these ornate vessels were affecting ship-decoration elsewhere. Galleys were used, it is true, in the Baltic also, but there climatic conditions had discouraged superfluous ornament, and they had practically none to impart. The tendency in all countries, France included, was now towards the suppression of carved figures, however, and by the middle of the century, or a little later, we find rococo on the wane and more economical plain mouldings or applied balusters forming the greater part of the decoration of all ships; wreaths around ports, cherubs, and mermaids had gone from them; a figure-head, even, gave place to a shield or a fiddle-head in some, and the flowering-time of the decorated ship was almost over.

In rig, the most notable innovation, coming in very early in the 18th century, is the jib, set on a new spar, the jib-boom. This spar was at first carried at the side of the bowsprit, and pointing through the spritsail top that, with its mast and sail, survived for some years after the jib came into fashion. Later this top was reduced to a couple of B-shaped projections, "the bees of the bowsprit," and the spritsail-topmast became a mere "jack-staff." In English ships the jib-boom lay on top of the bowsprit and was given a perpendicular cap at the bowsprit-end on which this jack-staff was fixed; in others the jib-boom stayed beside the bowsprit longer, given a

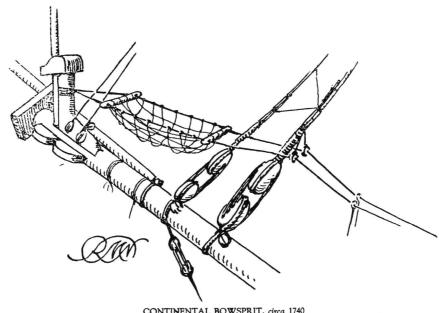

CONTINENTAL BOWSPRIT, *circa* 1740

cap that was set askew, for the old knee of the spritsail-topmast, though made smaller, kept its place as a support for the jackstaff and also for the little netting in which the furled fore-topmast stay-sail lay like a swaddled babe in a hammock. With the loss of the spritsail-topmast the spritsail-topsail found a new home, beneath the jib-boom. Beyond this a separate flying jib-boom with its sail was added later, and below the bowsprit-end a dolphin-striker. Other changes to note are the introduction of a pair of boomkins

56

with blocks for the fore-tacks, thus severing their old connection with the beak (an extension of the single *chique*, that had survived in small beakless vessels), and the addition of reefs to the courses (doing away with bonnets) as well as to the topsails. Studding-sails and royals also became general. The stays of the mainmast were still used, as to the slightest possible extent they are yet, for the attachment of braces, but in the first half of the century these braces were led further aft, and the bowlines were at the same time led further forward, leaving the stays almost clear. Until nearly the middle of the century the mizen in all large ships was still a lateen. Influenced by the example of the hoy's mainsail, however, the ship of that time sacrificed the part of that sail lying before the

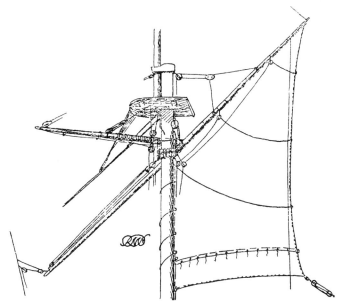

HALF MIZEN, WITH LATEEN YARD RETAINED

mast, lacing the remainder to the mast, but keeping the lateen yard whole as a help in balancing the peak by its weight, and as an attachment for the mizen-bowlines, still thought indispensable. In smaller ships a gaff mizen like the mainsail of a brigantine was already carried, but the full lateen mizen was still kept in others, being retained by the French long after the English had given it up.

Tops in the early years of the century ceased to be round, their after part becoming square and thus making a better spread for the topmast shrouds. They had already flattened out until it was difficult to see in them the descendants of the bowl-like 16th-century and earlier tops, but they still kept, radiating from their midst, the vestiges of the knees that had supported their high sides, and they continued to keep these after this change of shape, though eventually a grating replaced the old solid platform. Another vestige of old ways was the top-armour, a piece of red cloth or painted canvas that covered a netting held on a stanchion-supported rail at its aft-side. These, of course, balanced the waist-cloths and boarding-nettings, later used as hammock nettings, along the sides of the ship herself, but it is strange, after all this addition of masts and sails, to find in them yet so close a parallel to the "castles" and "top-castle" of the middle ages. The main top, the old "top-castle," was, when an admiral or commodore was aboard, given a further likeness to the poop or "after-castle," by being given a top-lantern exactly matching the three poop-lanterns. Although the crow-foot was almost forgotten in other uses, the top-crowfoot, introduced late in the 17th century, still rose from a "euphroe," Dutch *juffer*, on the stay beneath, to spread on the top-rim, keeping the foot of a topsail from fretting or hitching there, until the end of the 18th. It was still easy to tell an English or American rigged vessel from another by the form of the caps through most of the century. Another little distinction was that in English ships the mizen-topsail braces, until about the middle of the century, still led aft to the peak of the mizen yard; but in others ran forward to the after shroud of the main rigging, crossing one another, so that all the yards could be braced from one side of the ship.

Coming to the 19th century we have, as its chief features, a suppression of the ornamental parts of a ship and an expansion of its sail area. Early in the century the sunk beak-head was exchanged for bows that rose rounded to the upper deck level, the hollow of the head-rails being filled with a straight head-board. The only other striking change of form was made by the later introduction of the "circular" stern; practical, but unlovely. The removal of the wales, that for most of the 18th century had still emphasised the curves of a ship's sheer, had paved the way for a new method of planking and of painting that laid stress not on the ship but on her armament. The decks, with their guns, had long run almost straight from end to end of the ship, the portholes cutting into the wales where these came in their way, and once these guiding lines were removed the natural curve of the ship ceased to decide the

58

lines of the planking, these following the deck line instead. The ideal of a sheerless ship had been adopted, and to emphasise this new straightness came the fashion of painting the sides black, with a white line along each battery; the portlids being made conspicuous as black on white, the whole giving an air of Sabbatical respectability, like that of black frock-coat and top-hat relieved by snowy linen. Small sympathy with mere art was to be expected from those who approved of such a painting, that ignored the form of the ship painted, and decoration was henceforth confined to a little vestigial carved work astern, in which originality was severely checked, and an apology for a scroll beneath the figure head, on which the ship-carver was forced to concentrate his artistic efforts.

Fashions at sea were still until the middle of the century set for European merchant ships chiefly by their navies, and the smart frigates in this new painting were speedily imitated by the warlike East Indiamen that carried guns, and then by other merchantmen that, carrying none, sported the even less commendable row of "painted ports." This painting of sham ports was actually a revival, partly with the same object of frightening possible enemies, of a custom that had been in vogue with Hanseatic hulks in the 16th century; in its later phases, however, the ports assumed a sloping form that could deceive nobody, and were painted on craft of all sorts, even barges, open seine-boats, and in at least one instance, at Teignmouth, on one-man-power ferry-boats. However false in itself, this "frigate" style of painting, in which a ship was made inconspicuous as compared with her row of guns, real or imaginary, yet had the merit of setting off well the cloud of canvas that she bore; the hull becoming in effect rather like the body that just serves to hold together the glorious wings of a butterfly, and proving how difficult it is to make a sailing ship other than beautiful.

The sails were now being cut flatter, this leading eventually to the disuse of bowlines, and were bent to a jackstay at the top of the yard, hiding this from sight as viewed from the lee-side. The boomless mizen with its yard had universally given place to one with gaff and boom early in the century, and during the middle years of it similarly shaped but boomless trysails were commonly added on the main and fore masts. One sail, the old spritsail, was dropped early in the century. Its yard, still found useful as a spreader of rigging, was later divided into two "spritsail gaffs," these

59

in turn surviving on many bows as "whiskers" of iron. Another alteration in rigging was that of bringing the futtock-shrouds in to the mast instead of setting them up to the main rigging.

Although in Europe, except for a few Dutch "flights," and the "pink-ships" and "whalers" that followed their example, the man-of-war had still been setting the fashion for "frigate-built" merchant ships, by the middle of the century the Americans, developing the whaler and the trader on lines of their own, had produced a new type, the clipper, that owed little to naval ideals, and was imitated by British builders. Her length and fineness of lines were her own, but her small doubled channels seem to have been invented to leave space for the hoisting of a whaler's many boats. Boat-davits were similarly used on all whalers long before they were adopted in other ships. It was seldom that the clipper, even when English, wore the "painted ports" in flattering imitation of the frigate, being content to look what she was—the fastest, not the best armed, ship that had ever sailed the seas. Now again in such ships a more artistic emphasis was laid on the beauty of their own lines by such slight decoration as they received. A circular stern, without cabin lights, and with the merest vestige of scroll-work to represent the lost quarter galleries, and, forward, a little suggestion of a beak with a figure-head or fiddle-head, sufficed. To have given more would have been as out of place as to cover a racehorse with the trappings of the tilt-yard. For twenty years or more these fine yacht-like ships raced across the seas, piling on not only some "flying kites" that disappeared with them, but also, for economy's sake, splitting up the greater sail areas of their canvas into inner and outer jibs, and upper and lower topsails. Then steam, with the opening of the Suez Canal, took the trade of the British clipper, while iron construction soon put the American wooden ship out of the running. Thus was brought about a new and slower type of merchant ship—"the clipper clipped." Not the frigate, nor the ocean racer set the fashion now, even for sailing ships, for these grew more like steamships. Square bilged, wall-sided, built of iron, and later of steel, given a bridge amidships, with masts and spars of steel tubing, wire-rigged, and with steam donkey-engines, the later 19th-century sailing-ship had little in common with the older save what remained of her canvas. The old clipper, with her foremast set well inboard, had a long bowsprit to balance this, and her mainmast stood well above the others; the steel ship, four or five masted, with most of her masts alike, and with double top-gallant sails almost as big as her double topsails, had lost the traditional pyramidal sail-plan completely and taken one nearly rectangular. Conservatism still assigns to such a ship a modified clipper bow, sometimes even the painted ports of the frigate, and often a wood-carved figure-head. This decoration seems a mere pretence that the ship herself is still of wood, however—a borrowing of timber finery as a poor substitute for the as yet unfound decoration that belongs of right to the steel built sailing-ship—and quite justly as little of it is added as may serve to satisfy the convention. With auxiliary motor power, and every "labour-saver" that can be thought of, a few such big sailing ships, square-rigged as well as schooners, still hold their own, keeping, in spite of its curtailment, some of the beauty of sail; we even have some humbler craft, timber-built, timber-sparred, hemp-rigged, and still relying wholly on wind and man power, that struggle, more or less successfully, for existence, but the modern world has, on the whole, decided against the sailing-ship, great or small.

Such, briefly, are the chief changes in full-rigged ships from the days of "one ship, one sail" up (or down) to those of the five-master, in whose full suit of canvas that original sail—the mainsail—is but as one brick in a wall. To have gone fully into detail, even as it applies to model-making alone, would have filled an enormous book—hull-construction, spars, decks and deck-fittings, kevels, capstans, binnacles and steering-gear, rigging and blocks, sails and rigs, carved work and painting, flags, anchors, guns, each of these would have required a chapter, if not a volume, to do it justice— yet my hope is that this may serve as an introduction not only to the models that follow but to the fascinating study of wooden ships and their sails in times past, a study so neglected that it is still open to everyone to make in it some real discovery.

For sails and wooden ships in the present time the best that can be hoped is that somewhere on this earth they may find a place where they shall be allowed to keep alive their long-descended tradition of sea-craft, until some turn of fortune shall cause the world to need them again, and so set them once more on a career of development from form to form. What new shapes they may take is for us quite unimaginable, but if we may judge of their future by their past we may be sure that none of them can fail of beauty.

ENGLISH SHIP, END OF 16th CENTURY, AFTER RAWLINSON MS.

62

NOTES ON THE MODELS ILLUSTRATED.

Frontispiece. This model is based on the previously described print by "W.A." Note the steep-tub on the quarter, for unsalting meat, part of the shifter's duty being to get into the tub and tread the salt out; the boat, which in being raised or lowered by the tackles passes just where the skids are placed, showing their use as protecting the side; the cargo-port, used long before gun-ports; the craneline bags or "pokes," their mouths distended by hoops; the bowsprit grapnel; the guns, mounted on the aftercastle, and one in the mizen-top, and the top-netting shown on the fore-top, where also is placed a huge dart intended when cast down to pierce the bottom of an attacking galley. The blocks are all without strops, like those of galleys.

Pl. 1. This gives us Church-ships, votive and commemorative, *in situ*, the best possible way in which they can be seen. Carpaccio gives us two great ships, or carracks, and a galley, all of *circa* 1500, and thus fairly new when painted. With them are numberless other votive offerings, candles, flags, etc. Well as Carpaccio shows the decorative value of ship models, this is even more delight-fully seen in the interior of the Groote Kerk at Haarlem, the models of which are described elsewhere. The lantern-like object at the bow of the largest ship is one of the "Castles of Damietta," chained to another on the other side. The middle ship is shown in Plate 15. The hoy, or galiot, is given the lateen mizen that was later exchanged for a gaff sail. Her spritsail is set, and like the English hoy, Plate 69, she has no leeboard.

Pl. 2. This ship's underbody is but a gold cup, but the detachable upper part is close enough to the "W.A." carrack to merit a place among models. The dragon figure-head in "W.A.'s" print is exactly the same as the gargoyles given by him to his architectural subjects and not necessarily a close copy: here it is greatly exaggerated in size. Guns are added at the forecastle, which like the after-castle is far more ornate than "W.A.'s." The cargo-port is copied, chased on the surface, as a hinged door. The rigging is merely set up with toggles to holes in the sides. The craneline-bags have closed mouths and the single top-cranes are set, wrongly, before the tops. The form of the blocks is interesting, so also is the crew in varied dress and pose. As usual in later "nefs," a banquet is in progress on the poop.

Pl. 3. No very precise description of this great ship, whose building "wasted all the woods of Fife," and that, when built "cumbered all Scotland to put her to sea," is in existence. Mr. Patterson in making this "reconstruction" was guided by that of Lindesay of Pitscottie, and by some drawings supplied by myself, largely a matter of deduction, since no detailed ship-picture of this date is known, though there are earlier and later drawings which supply the loss to some extent. The forecastle is still of the 15th-century form; the poop is more solid, and over-hangs above the outligger and the square-tuck stern. The spritsail is stowed against the forecastle and the fore-tacks lead to a boomkin, which may have appeared in large vessels by this time. There are two mizens, the smaller of which, the "bonaventure," is here rigged galley-fashion. The gun-ports are a recent addition at this date. Nettings are shown defending the waist and "castles."

Pl. 4. This, as already stated, is of doubtful origin, but in many particulars conforms to one's expectations of what a church-ship of *circa* 1525 would be. The absence of guns would suggest, were it not for the shape of the stern, a date still earlier, *cf.* Carpaccio's ships, Plate 1.

Pl. 5. Comparison of this Venetian ship with Jal's drawing brings out, as already noted, some instances of "restoration." The backstays and the over-large rudder may be added to those mentioned.

Pl. 6. The drawings of Le Testu have given most of the information needed for the form and rigging of this model, which, as intended to hang, is left solid. Note the half-top on the mizen-mast and the shields on the after sides of the tops. The topsails are still small, and the fore-tacks lead to a boomkin, the *chique.* The martnetts are conspicuous, rising from the lower yards, as in W.A.'s carrack and in prints after Bruegel.

Pl. 7. This is finished in more detail than the last, and shows amongst other things the method of furling topsails that remained usual for over a century (see Plate 85), and the open gallery, with arched timbers leading from it to the ship's side (see note to Plate 80). The spritsail is still furled alongside of the beak. The martnetts now hang in festoons below the furled sails; the ensign-staff is fixed at the corner of the poop, as in Plate 6, and again in Plate 19.

Pl. 8. Adding to the previous description of this model, one may note the decoration of warriors and tritons on the sides and galleries. Open port-lids are represented by crudely cut lions' heads, and a lion forms the figure-head. The carving is thickly covered with paint, but the monogram, "C.4," is plainly visible on the taferel. A curious point in the 18th-century rigging is that the jib-stay is interrupted by being set up separately to and from the spritsail-topmast head, suggesting that the rigger worked from a misunderstood drawing. The mizen is also given a gaff instead of the expected lateen yard.

Pls. 9 *and* 10. This is especially valuable for its finely executed detail. The rigging is sadly disordered, but a comparison of its crowfoot work with that of the diagram already given will explain most of it. The high, square-rigged main-mizenmast is unique, but a lateen mizen-yard may formerly have been present also, and it is not even sure how much the rigging may have been "restored" in former times. The blocks are mostly unstropped, the deadeyes heart-shaped, and the caps open before. The decoration is most elaborate, the openwork between the two tiers of guns and along the long, round-ended gallery being very delicate. The hull is covered with bands of painted ornament, one repeating the Burgundy *briquet* badge. The streamers also show the Pillars of Hercules and the " ragged staff "cross of Burgundy, other heraldic emblems of Spanish rule in the Netherlands.

Pl. 11. On the stern and sails are the dates, 1603, 1715, and 1822, of its making and of later renovations. The latter have not added much beyond a few sails easily distinguished from the old ones, of which some, as notably the main topsail, set as foresail, are misplaced; and the whole requires little more than sorting out to restore it. The caps, open before; topmast, lashed, and heart-shaped deadeyes, outside the channels, are like those of the Madrid galleon, but

64

the blocks are all stropped. The bowsprit, stepped amidships, has apparently had a spritsail-topmast. The hull, if lacking in underbody, has truthful detail. The aftermost porthole is dropped to the level of the stern ports, cutting through the wale. Besides the chess-tree for the main-tack, there is a lead for the fore-tack in the head-rails and another for the main sheet over the forward edge of the gallery. The cathead is placed at the lowest point of the curve of the head-rails, as in the Madrid ship. Kevels are fixed against the rails at the waist, which has a grating. The anchors are original, the crew, like the poop-lantern, is of 1822, but may be substituted for an older one. The *Francis of Fowey* had a crew, and so has the Nuremberg cup, Plate 2. Crews, even for 18th- and 19th-century models, *e.g.*, Plate 91, are not uncommon. The designs painted on the sails are different on each side, and include: Mercury, a Mermaid, a Pelican, the Sun, the Moon, the arms of the Peller family, and a portrait, presumably of the owner or donor of the ship.

Pls. 12 and 13. Mr. C. E. G. Crone has given us in this model a scientific reconstruction of an 80-ton *jacht* of the Dutch East India Company that is far more perfect in detail than the full-sized reconstruction of 1909, and cannot differ in any important degree from the actual *Halve Maen*, of which no plans exist. Being a small vessel, this has no gallery, no spritsail-topmast, and no round "tops gallant." The mizen half-top is made barrel-shaped, following some old Dutch prints. The spritsail is furled out on the bowsprit, but the foretacks still lead to a boomkin, and the bowsprit is set to starboard. The flags, painting, and crew are all equally realistic and correct, making this a most delightfully thorough contribution to history. See *Mariner's Mirror*, 1922, p. 265.

Pl. 14. From the keel up to the white bulwarks this is mainly original, though the feminine figure-head is apparently substituted for one more characteristic of the period. The hull is very deficient in beam, as well as in depth. The tutelary Virgin and Child, in high relief, occupy the taferel, but the roof of the lower gallery is continued astern below the figures, a most unusual arrangement. Apart from the galleries and turrets, the most interesting feature is perhaps the row of lion-faces, not on the portlids, but between them. The after-ports cut into the wales, but are not sunk. The heart-shaped deadeyes may survive from the old rigging, which probably included two mizens. The foremast is stepped abaft the beakhead-bulkhead, and the bowsprit is amidships; both apparently in their original positions.

Pl. 15. This is the middle, and oldest ship, of the three shown in Plate 1. The hull is deficient in beam and underbody, but otherwise is faithful to fact. The masts, tops, and open caps are all original, as is also the bowsprit, stepped amidships, but the rigging was evidently overhauled in 1686, the position of the lifts of the lower yards being alone sufficient to show this. The mizen-topsail, topgallantsail, and spritsail are furled, the other sails are stiffened with wire and painted. The arms of Holland are painted on the taferel, and crossed guns and swords along the quarter; the painting on the poop and gallery is still of 16th-century style. A roughly cut lion forms the figure-head. A grating is shown over the waist. The larger and later model is far more crudely designed than this, though it has, for a church ship, very good rigging detail.

Pl. 16. Though put together here as showing the effect of hanging town-hall models *in situ*, these are all of different periods, the first alone being of a date *circa* 1625-1630. The second, of *circa* 1640, with closed gallery, shows the lack of beam characteristic of such models. The metal guns are clamped on from outside in an unsightly way, rather spoiling the beauty of both these Bremen ships. The third is a very well-finished late 18th-century specimen of the hanging model. The fourth, from Emden, is an equally good ship of the end of the 17th century.

Pls. 17 *and* 18. In making this, the most ambitious piece of reconstruction yet attempted in any country, Mr. Henry B. Culver has been guided chiefly by the print of the ship by Payne, the stern view of her in a portrait of Peter Pett serving to eke this out, and correcting the imaginary stern that had been given to her by a previous reconstuctor. As a "ship royal" this is more elaborately rigged than was usual at the time, and Van Dyck is claimed as the designer of her decorations. The minute way in which every detail of these elaborations is carried out is a strong feature of the model.—See *Mariner's Mirror*, 1922, p. 367. Plate 18 shows, from this ship, the characteristic English beakhead of the time in its most ornate form. The comb for the fore-tacks is carved as a serpent. Note the shroud-like gammoning of the bowsprit, shown not only in Payne's print, but also in drawings of ships by Van de Velde the elder, at the Rijks Museum, Amsterdam.

Pl. 19. Finished in 1654 by Jacob Jensen, instructor in ivory work to King Frederick III. of Denmark, this model may have been long in making. The ship represented was built by Daniel Sinclair twenty years earlier, and the extreme sheer and much crowfooted rigging suggests that earlier period, though the monogram of King Frederick III. 1648-1670, is on the main topsail. The gallery is open for a short distance, the ensign-staff is still at a corner of the poop, a grating runs over the waist, the bowsprit is to starboard and a chained grapnel still hangs at its end. The deadeyes are still almost heart-shaped, and the high catheads are like those of contemporary English ships. The rigging details, in silver wire, are of great value; they have been subjected to some ignorant "repair," but this is too obvious to be very misleading.

Pl. 20. This most picturesque model shows the round stern that characterised the flight or *fluitschip*—a survival of the round stern of 15th-century Low Country vessels like those of Memlinc or "W.A." An excellent example, allowing for changing fashions of just such a vessel, was engraved by Frans Huys in 1565, after Bruegel. This has on its stern the date 1564, and the establishment of the flight as a type dates from near that time. Flights, built larger and more heavily armed, were used in the Mediterranean and East India trades. This one is probably a Baltic or Norway trader. Though given a spritsail-topsail she has no mizen topsail, and is very lightly armed. Later flights are shown in plates 40, 50, and 106.

Pl. 21. This model was found in a warehouse of the Dutch East India Company at Middelburg, in its present unrestored state. Though an East India-man, the *Prins Willem* differed from contemporary ships of war chiefly in lacking a forecastle, and actually took part in the battle off the Kentish Knock in 1652. The model is remarkable for its fine workmanship, especially notable in the stern carvings, with a figure of William II. of Orange, the arms of Middleburg and Zeeland, and the monogram "V.O.C.M.", meaning "United East India Company,

66

Middelburg (Chamber)." The decks, as is shown by the guns, are made to curve with the wales; those of the gun-room and cabin alone being horizontal. The rigging is not quite contemporary, as is proved by the position of the lifts, the vangs on the mizen yard, and the reef in the mizen. The top-armings and the half-furled sails give rarely-seen details. The waistboard pierced for musketry, and the clinker "cage-work" are characteristic. The beak is longer, and the sheer greater, in this most graceful vessel than in any ships of the next decade.

Pl. 22. The original *Amaranthe* model is stored rather than exhibited, at Stockholm, awaiting the building of a Naval Museum there. This is an exact replica, made for the museum at Gothenburg, and shows the very minutely exact way in which the original is rigged.—See *Mariner's Mirror*, 1913, p. 204. The decks here are nearly horizontal, the ports, as in the Dutch ships that follow, cutting the wales. Dutch influence is very strongly shown throughout.

Pls. 23, 24 and 25. The name *Hollandia* has been suggested for this ship, and also that of *Zeven Provincien*; she does not, however, match what is known of either of these ships. The hull, as compared with that of an English or even a Swedish ship, is contrived to draw little water, suiting the Dutch shallows. Every detail, even to the interior cabin fittings, is given exactly in this model, the sails of which have been added. The waist-grating has rails, as in a similar model at Ghent; the lion figure-head is typically Dutch of the period, and the beautifully executed stern carvings show the arms of Orange surrounded by the English order of the Garter. The model is possibly one presented to Prince William in 1666 by the Admiralty of Amsterdam. The double *slingerlijst* astern may date it as up to ten years later than 1660.

Pl. 26. An uninstructed attempt at representing a ship built according to Dutch ideals. The guns are very insistent, but there is some reasonably good detail in spite of the lack of proportion, and the character is well kept, if caricatured.

Pl. 27. An unusually good church-ship, in quite fair proportion except at the head. Since I saw this model, she has been very carefully restored by Mr. J. W. Van Nouhuys, Director of the Prins Hendrik Museum. The restorations, made from contemporary authorities, include all the rigging, the rails of the head, and the top of the stern, which had been clumsily renovated in 18th-century taste. The painted wave-line is also a restoration. On the stern is painted her name, with the date 1662. She has some points in common with the Dutch church ship hulk in Paris, but is earlier, and quite different astern.

Pl. 28. This very beautiful model was formerly at Ghent, where there still remains another superb Dutch model of about the same date. The original stern had been removed, and that of the *Hollandia*, which ship the model otherwise resembles, has now been substituted by Mr. C. E. G. Crone for the incongruous one that replaced it. The rigging is also a restoration. Ships of this class were the largest then built in Holland.

Pl. 29. This wrecked model, named "Bristol, 1666" in a doubtful inscription on the stern, is a very early example of a ship with oar-ports. Mr. R. C. Anderson, *Mariner's Mirror*, 1922, p. 364, offers the suggestion that it represents a merchant-ship fitted for oars, of the type called "galley," in the late 17th and early 18th centuries.

Pl. 30. This is the earliest of a series of fine English models, several of which are here shown in a similar position, making it easy to note the gradual change in shipbuilding style during the next half-century. Here the great height astern, apparently serving only for parade, is very noticeable, linking this to earlier ships. The contrast between this and the contemporary Dutch vessels in shape and decoration is a striking one.

Pl. 31. Above is shown, on a larger scale, the typical head and decoration of the time—the figures along the bulkhead, the port-wreaths and the painted trophies, the equestrian figure-head and many caryatides. The cathead has the star decoration still so often seen there. As we have seen, *jacht* in Dutch could be used of trading ships like the *Half Moon*, and not only of such ornate craft of state as is shown below, that were hoys in rig but miniature ships in build. The term came into English from Holland, with the type, after the middle of the 17th century. Though sometimes a ketch, sometimes ship-rigged, the yacht remained in England a vessel of state and pleasure, but in Norway and Denmark the *jagt* is a little square-tucked coaster. Like *chasse marée* and " ketch," the name implies a vessel used for " chasing."

Pl. 32. This very beautiful model of a richly decorated English ship has been re-rigged in a fashion which could now be improved upon. As compared with the earlier ship, Plate 30, the stern is much lower, though still high. Both ships have an elaborate entry-port on the starboard side, and their quarter-galleries and other decorations are similar.

Pl. 33. This shows the yacht in her hoy rig (*cf.* Plate 69). The model originally had the unusual feature of sails, the boltropes of which alone remained when Mr. Anderson undertook her restoration. The yards are not well seen in the photograph, but she carried a square topsail like that in Plate 89.

Pl. 34. This fine piece of reconstruction shows how much Danish ship-builders had by this time got away from Dutch models. The present ship shows French rather than other influence in the form and decoration of the stern, with a return to open galleries of the type that became usual in the 18th century. The port-lids painted with the national *Dannebrog* colours will be seen again in later Danish ships.

Pl. 35. The *Albemarle* shows the long rake forward of her time (all the better perhaps because of the missing head-rails), balanced by the considerable sheer, and the high stern. The English Royal Yacht gives more cabin-room than usual, the after ports are blocked up, with carved flowers within the port-wreath.

Pl. 36. There is some later work in the bulwarks aft, and on the stern itself. The name *Die Hoffnung* is very large, and not perhaps original. The rigging has been renovated in places, the sails included. A waist-board, pierced for musketry, is still carried.

Pl. 37. Another superb English model, showing in many ways the gradual settling down into 18th-century form. The skids at the waist are a new feature.

Pl. 38. As compared with the *Christianus Quintus*, this Danish ship is far less unlike a Dutch one. The name-board with *Urania* is 19th-century, as are also the gallows-bitts before the main mast, the sails, and most of the rigging. The inscription below records a personal name only, but is interesting as such. The growing size of the false stern, making here one convex curve from keel to lion, is a late 17th-century trait, exaggerated in the church-ships, Plates 48 and 49. A date, 1719, on the stern, seems too late to be original.

Pl. 39. This is the only known model of a 17th-century Dutch three-decker. But few of them were built, this one probably representing the *West Friesland.* Though not built to scale the model is good in detail, and Mr. Anderson has been as careful in giving her the Dutch rig of her time as in rigging the many fine English models restored by him. The ship is practically a built-up two-decker, giving her a very high beakhead-bulkhead. Note, in this and other foreign ships, the higher position of the channels as compared with their place in English ones.

Pl. 40. This shows how closely the Dutch fashions were copied in Lübeck in 1690, the date on the stern of this flight, a larger and later specimen of the type shown in Plate 20. In England the " coal-cat," later becoming the collier-brig; the " pink," and the whaler, showed copies almost as close of the Dutch round-sterned fly-boats and flights.

Pl. 41. Though given an incongruous rudder and a clumsy head, this, for a church-ship, is unusually well proportioned. A gold swan is carved on the stern, and the name is apparently that of an actual ship. The guns are small rather than large, but the blocks are, as usual, oversized The rigging, though badly disarranged, is original. The spritsail-yard has wandered to the top of the bowsprit, and the mizen yard is missing. The running rigging is sadly messed up, and she was always given a short allowance of shrouds.

Pl. 42. This is the most magnificent specimen of 17th-century French model-making, and almost the only one that exists. It is complete in every detail except those of the sails, showing many typically French features. The short bowsprit and mizen-mast increase the unlikeness to either English or Dutch ships. The stern carvings are rich in the extreme, with open galleries of the later style. The upper ports are arched and lidless, and four skids are present at the waist.

Pl. 43. A typical English ship of her class. The bowsprit is here given no round-top.

Pl. 44. A fine specimen of English ship-carving. The stern is still divided by continuous lines of brackets and pilasters, but now has an open gallery added. The panels between the carved work are painted, the monogram, " W.M.R.," and the portraits of William and Mary being conspicuous The channels of the period are well seen here.

Pl. 45. The cause of the dilapidation of this beautiful wreck has been already stated. Finished in great detail, she is somewhat like the *Royal Louis;* she has arched ports at the poop only, however, and her bowsprit and mizen-mast are less unusually proportioned.

Pl. 46. The upper picture shows the ship of Plate 44 in another aspect. An entry-port is now placed on the larboard side also. The lower picture shows how the same sort of work was adapted to a smaller ship. The port-wreaths and dotted star decoration, seen in the yachts of *circa* 1670, still hold their popularity.

69

Pl. 47. This shows various foreign influences in which the French predominates. Round ports are still given to the half-deck. The rigging is unfinished, and there are no guns, but there is much good detail. The date of the model is likely to be nearer to 1720 than to 1691.

Pl. 48. A grotesque, but correctly detailed, church ship. The port-lids are left out to make room for the enormous guns. The rigging is original, and almost untouched, but the hoisted yards suggest that sails were there formerly. Invisible here, on the stern is the lion of Norway, with its curved-handled axe.

Pl. 49. Though Genoese, this church-ship is remarkably like the last in some ways, but is more completely rigged. Although, as in the Bergen ship, the lower yards are fitted with jears, the caps are still open before, and the topmasts lashed, as in ships of the beginning of the century. Note the elaborate setting up of the fore-topmast stay. Dutch rather than French influence is shown in the decorations.

Pl. 50. Most ships of unknown origin are called *Lion* simply because they have the usual lion at the head. This is perhaps more justly named so. Its chief interest is that it is a very unusually large specimen of the flight. The little gallery astern is, I believe, unique. The rigging and painting are modern. The lower ports cut the wale all along and the upper ones break up the channels, as in the *Hoffnung*.

Pl. 51. *La Réale* shows the Latin-type galley in all her glory. Beautiful as galleys were, it is impossible to forget how all this gorgeousness of gilded carving, painting, tilts, and banners, only made more conspicuous the misery of their rowers, condemned innocents and kidnapped redskins, under Colbert's relentless rule mixed with captives and criminals, and chained to their benches. The Venetian trading galeass is of happier associations. She is without her three lateen-rigged masts, her oars, and her rudder, and her bow and stern both imitate current ship fashions, but she enables one to imagine the beauty of the galeasses that came to England and Flanders in the 15th century "wel ladene wyth thynges of complacence."

Pl. 52. Seen from above, this shows a little of the diagonally arranged benches with the *coursie* running down the middle. The guns are all forward under the *rambade*. The poop, in older galleys a mere tilt-frame, is here solid. The mizen-mast is also a new feature, added only in the largest galleys. The *calcet* mast-head blocks, and shroudless rigging set up with tackles, *couladou*, in Latin style, are clearly seen.

Pl. 53. To the details of deck-arrangement and display given before, this adds the striped sails with their *orses*, *ostes*, and other running rigging. The *rambade* is here, as in another Maltese galley at the Science Museum, given an embrasured defence like the mediaeval "castles." Note the grapnels as anchors, the very long beak, and, aft of the *apostis* on which the oars rest, the curved accommodation-ladder that is usually raised when not in use.

Pl. 54. This ship may be compared with that in Plate 43. A jib-boom appears here for the first time, but there are anomalies in the rigging that deprive this of authority.

70

Pl. 55. This shows more correctly than the last the current leads of rigging; except for the stern, the galleries of which are of a less usual form, the ships are very similar.

Pls. 56 and 57. The intimate view of the *Britannia's* decks aft—not completely planked, so as to show the construction—shows how far the enrichment of a great ship of 1700 was carried. With it all, the back of the carved timber of the taferel is left like the back of a carved chair or mirror of the time, its pierced parts simply chamfered off. The way in which the curves of the staircase rails are made to interplay with those of the ship's rail is very pleasing. Plate 57 shows the stern, still keeping much of the 17th-century English convention, but given two open galleries, the lower of which is extended to the quarter. The fighting cavaliers as design are more successful than the rather distorted figures at the corners. The royal arms and the three interlaced anchors of the Admiralty ornament the galleries, and a lion's head still, as in earlier ships, forms the rudder-head. Below is the bow with its equestrian head. The bitts and timber-heads are all given carved heads. Those at each side of the bowsprit are still perpetuated in the modern use of the term " knighthead."

Pls. 58, 59 and 60. The finest of the wonderful Cuckfield collection of models, this *St. George* is finished in fullest detail, and is a perfect record of contemporary rigging. The hull shows a further movement towards 18th-century ideals, but is still as splendidly decorated as ever. The fish-davit is rigged out ready to fish the anchor, and the smallest details are everywhere perfectly rendered. The mizen-topmast stay still branches on to the main shrouds, and the mizen stay is given an unusual crowfoot tackle like that of the mizen lift. In plate 59 we have a closer view of the decks and quarter. The back of the carved taferel is here itself carved. The entry-port, with its balustrade, comes right on to the channel as in earlier ships. Plate 60 gives us the finely composed figure-head of St. George and the Dragon, and such details as the stowing of the anchors, the " horse in the head " with its deadeyes and lanyard and the fore-tack, led in now at a hole in the middle rail. Particularly interesting is the main-top, too, with all its surroundings.

Pl. 61. This church-ship, from Öckerö, an island near Gothenburg, has a formless hull that is possibly an altered 16th-century one, but whatever its age, the rigging seems likely to be somewhat later, of *circa* 1740; the caps, though rounded above, are set alongships in the English fashion. The rigging is unusually full and good for a church-ship, and makes the lack of detail elsewhere more conspicuous. The topmasts are impossibly tall.

Pl. 62. Here the 18th century asserts itself still more strongly than in previous English ships. The sheer is markedly less, and the lessened height aft corresponds. The channels are lifted to a position above the middle tier of ports, at last imitating foreign example. The upper ports are without wreaths, and the carved work greatly reduced.

Pls. 63, 64 and 65. The quarter-deck guns alone have wreaths, and though enrichment lingers plain mouldings are on the way. The sheer and forward rake grow less. The lower picture in plate 64 shows the supports for " waist cloths " fore and aft, though not in the waist from which they first took their name. Plate 65 shows the great variety of stern design that could be given to ships of the English fleet at this transitional time. The arcading on the counter of the middle one, repeated at her beakhead-bulkhead, is almost Elizabethan, while above it are pilasters suggestive of the later 18th century. The carving everywhere is rather an ornamentation of a space left plain by the ship-designer, than part of an ornamentally designed ship.

Pl. 66. Two interesting smaller vessels. The top one was probably rigged as a snow, and is rather yacht-like in her proportions. The *Carolina* is larger but more definitely a yacht.

Pls. 67 and 68. The addition of sails makes this the most complete English model of so early a date. The hull is now definitely of the 18th-century form, and the decoration is only a slightly more ornate version of the standard 18th-century mode. The so called " flying jib " on its jib-boom is now introduced, though not with the approval of Wm. Sutherland, who says of it that it is " a sail of good service to draw the ship forward, but very prejudicial to the wear of the ship . . . 'Tis used with a boom or small mast extended at the extremes of the bowsprit." Sutherland, *Shipbuilder's Assistant*, also named studding sails as in common use, but we as yet find no stunsail-booms fitted to models. The sails of this *Royal George* allow us to see the reefs, as yet but few, in the topsails. In the stern we already have the small gallery balusters and larger windows of later ships and the taferel is cut across with a fourth row of lights, while the old continuous lines of pilasters and brackets have quite gone.

Pl. 69. This shows the general appearance and rig of one of the commonest types of its period. Two 18th-century hoys turned into lightships seem to be the only contemporary models of these vessels—English translations of Dutch galliots like that at Haarlem, Plate 1. Originating as spritsail craft, these were given a " half-sprit " or gaff, a rig adopted for yachts like that of Plate 33. The round stern of the hoy, like that of the " pink," was given a very projecting "lute" aft, that resembled the stern of a galley more than that of the Dutch original.

Pls. 70 and 71. These ships, built, one on the establishment of 1706, the other on that of 1719, illustrate well the trend in shipbuilding. Port-wreaths are denied the latter; the head reaches the maximum of contraction, and the carving is diminished. The second is a notably detailed and well rigged model. Note the top-armings and main-top lantern.

Pls. 72, 73. These models, both remarkably fine specimens of the art, represent the same ship, in her re-built form of 1719. They differ, however, in one important item; the lower wales being separate in the rigged model and placed together in the other. This is interesting as dating the introduction of the joined wales in English ships, which seems likely to have taken place while the re-building was in progress. The skids are not fitted to the Greenwich model and there are other minor points of difference; one apparently being the project, and the other the final product. The tops now ceased to be round; a break with very old tradition.

Pl. 74. The upper ship, very handsome of body if less decorated, shows the new doubled wales of Plate 72. One is perhaps better able to judge of the beauty of this ship as a ship because the framing is not shown below. The lower ship shows a slight return to older fashions. She is given oar-ports, although a 60-gun ship. A sea-horse takes the place of the usual "lion."

Pl. 75. The now almost circular stern has greatly changed since the 17th century. The lowering and broadening astern has gone on as in English ships, but with other results, the curve of the *slingerlijst* still asserting itself, though the taferel, like the English one, has become a mere edging at the top of the stern. Over the tiller-hole are carved the arms of Batavia, the seat of Dutch government in the East Indies, a sword in pale within a wreath. The details of carving and the poop-lantern are still of 17th-century style. The *Padmos*, at Rotterdam, and other models at Dordrecht, show similar sterns.

Pl. 76. The lower wales are still separate, but all ports are square, and there is little carved work. The poles are those from which flags were flown at the launching ceremony.

Pl. 77. All ports square ; a doubled lower wale, and a "classical" stiffness in the quarter-galleries characterize this fine model. The spritsail-topmast is still of importance, and has its top. The entry-port is now beneath the fore-end of the main-channel.

Pl. 78. The lead of the fore-braces, further back on the stay, if of 1739, is a very early example, probably the rigging is nearer 1750 in date. The mizen is of the "brigantine" pattern, first introduced in ship-rig in smaller ships such as this. Hammock-nettings are shown. The topsails are close-reefed, and the topgallant-sails sent down and stowed in the rigging. The current severity of taste has affected the carved work, and the sheer is slight.

Pl. 79. Built in Holland, *circa* 1660, this was long the fastest ship afloat, easily making 16 knots. Chapman, the author of *Architectura Mercatoria Navalis* in whose English parentage we may take pride, lived as a child on board this ship when she was moored at Gothenburg, and a drawing of her then made by him still exists. From this, and plans in the book named above, this model was made, showing the ship, rebuilt, as Chapman knew her. The round ports were perhaps original : she is given oar-ports as well.

Pl. 80. Here the stern is less round than in *Den Ary*, Plate 75. The clinker-work above survives and the quarter-gallery is given a series of carved timbers that are elongated descendants of those seen above the open gallery in Plate 7. These survive on the gallery roof and appear again, in Plate 97, on a still later Dutch ship. The sails of this East Indiaman show us our first example of the cut-down mizen, with yard kept whole, and also of studding-sails. The spritsail-topmast has gone, but the spritsail-topsail is set on the jib-boom. Royals and a mizen-topgallantsail are shown, and three reefs to the topsails. The waist-cloth and waist-board pierced with musket-holes survive from the 17th century.

Pl. 81. Although Dutch, the decorations fore and aft are here French in type. The model is not built to an exact scale, but has much good detail.

Pl. 82. This shows, very beautifully, the current taste in decoration. The classical sculptures and the painted trophies and scroll-work survive from the

73

17th century, but the pilasters and balusters and the shell ornament over the light-ports on the quarter are quite of the period. The lower wales are separated.

Pl. 83. As compared with the last ship, one notices the disappearance of wooden statuary. The quarter gallery is surmounted by a clock-headed survival of the half-turrets of former days, but ends below in the same spiral that we have seen in English ships, beginning as a fish-tail in Plates 64 and 70. Stun'-sail booms are fitted, but no royals or mizen-topgallantsail is carried, and the mizen is a lateen.

Pl. 84. Lent to a marine painter who was told to " do what he liked with it," this model was returned in its present condition—an example of the small appreciation given by one artist to the work of one, perhaps better skilled, in another art. The result is at least picturesque and the wreck above emphasizes the beautiful and characteristically French work of her decorations. The upper-most ports, square below, are arched above in the older style. The rigging is contemporary, and beautifully executed.

Pl. 85. The general trend of sea-fashions affects all countries similarly. Thus in this and the last plate we see a doubled lower wale, as in the earlier English ships. Here the carved work astern is entirely Spanish in style, though the shapes that it decorates are suggested by French design. The upper deck ports are lidless. The realistic way in which the ship is " laid up " is very interesting. The rounded fronts of the topmast crosstrees are relics of the round top there. The knee of the old spritsail-topmast is still kept in its place, the bowsprit cap being set askew.

Pl. 86. This model, though finely finished and decorated, can hardly be built to scale. She seems impossibly dumpy as compared with the Swedish scale model in Plate 88, that represents a similar ship. The stowing of the sails, the topsails still " farthelled " as in the late 16th century, is excellently shown. The trophy-painted topsides are no longer clinker-worked, and the lion at the head and the galleries astern follow French models.

Pl. 87. This frigate has oar-ports, so low that some of them cut the doubled lower wale. The lateen, or lug, mizen-topsail yard is unique. There is a dolphin-striker on the bowsprit, suggesting a later date for at least this part of the rigging.

Pl. 88. This is not unlike the Dutch East Indiaman, Plate 86, in all but proportions. The shifting of the fore braces has by this time practically cleared the stays, giving a more modern appearance to the rigging.

Pl. 89. The Dutch yacht, by 1750, has changed little from that of 1650, except in the carved work. Leeboards were not wanted in the deeper-built English yacht and hoy, otherwise there is little difference between this and these of Plates 33 and 69. The Dutch gave the un-hoylike peak-halyards as seen here to 17th-century yachts also. The scarfed topmast is a mediaeval survival, and the stem-head still curves back as in the 15th-century fishing boats drawn by " W.A.", the stay being set up to it, by a lanyard passing through holes in it, a fashion imitated not only in the English yacht and hoy, but in later cutters. The wooden fenders are a Dutch contrivance, but rough log fenders of the same sort are still in temporary use in every harbour.

74

Pl. 90. One of the finest of French models, this is wonderfully complete in detail. The rigging and sails are a fine example of restoration. The stern decorations are here completely *rococo*, with little trace of older conventions.

Pl. 91. A block carved model with a wooden crew aboard, and with contemporary rigging and sails.

Pl. 92. 1775 is perhaps a little early for the precise rig of this reconstructed armed lugger. Lescallier gives no lugger in his *Vocabulaire*, 1777, and in his *Gréement des Vaisseaux*, 1791, gives one with squarer sails and without a mizen topsail. The rig originated in the English Channel, deriving from that of square-sailed fishing vessels of the "Biscay shallop" type. Armed luggers like this were used as despatch boats, revenue cruisers, smugglers, and privateers. The topmasts are fixed abaft the masthead, and the rigging is composed of runners and tackles instead of shrouds.

Pl. 93. The head is typically French, the forward rake being less than in English ships. A new thing here, and in Plate 90, is the doubled tack, the fore-tacks leading to blocks on boomkins. Bruegel's presumable model shows double tacks, but this is not confirmed elsewhere, and single tacks, made tapering, have hitherto been the rule. The half-mizen, with its lateen yard, is well seen, and also the boat hanging from the tackles. Davits as yet are confined to whale-ships.

Pl. 94. A specimen of Chapman's designs—an attempt to combine shallow draught with great speed. Crankiness was often a defect of this inventive designer's experimental ships. The topsails on each mast were common in schooners of this date. There is a canvas waist-cloth amidships, which when raised allows of oars being used. The schooner rig with square topsails on both masts was common until the 19th century, though now rarely seen.

Pl. 95. Here the mizen is a boomless trysail, much like that of the old hoy or yacht. The main and mizen channels are in one. The caps are made English-fashion, and the bowsprit cap is no longer set askew.

Pl. 96. Models of such smaller craft are proportionately rare. The mainmast of such a schooner would perhaps have had a square topsail also, for one commonly sees this in contemporary pictures. The little window on the quarter was in some such vessels a mere dummy—the quarter-badge—put there to satisfy those who missed the quarter gallery of bigger ships. The window originated in yachts, as in Plates 31, 33 and 89, long before.

Pl. 97. This is a beautifully rigged model, with every detail, to sails and painting, carefully worked out. She still has the characteristic Dutch quarter-gallery, and is given oar-ports.

Pl. 98. The upper wales are here doubled as well as the lower, but keep a considerable sheer. The rigging is not contemporary, but illustrates such, then, novelties as the gaff mizen and the dolphin-striker.

Pl. 99. Interesting as showing the persistence of the Latin tradition, even after galleys were given up, in a fighting ship. Some beautiful chebec models at the Musée de Marine, Paris, show that in France also they were valued. The shrouds here, as in modern Mediterranean lateeners, are not like the galley's *sarties*, but rigged *à colonne* i.e., with runners and tackles. The projection aft is not unlike the "lute" of an English pink or hoy. The beak imitates that of a galley and oar-ports are fitted between the gun-ports. The type has changed little since the 17th century.

Pl. 100. As in the English ship, Plate 98, the upper wales are doubled. No dolphin-striker is fitted, and the mizen still has a yard. The high-placed channels would at once distinguish this from an English ship.

Pl. 101. A reconstruction, from plans and paintings, of a snow; a vessel like a brig, but having a square mizen, and behind it a trysail with a slender mast of its own. The hull derives from the beakless flights, cats, and hulks of long before, but the stern is not made round after the Dutch fashion.

Pl. 102. Interesting as being probably the oldest existing model made in America. Though not markedly unlike an English ship of her class, she already has a hint of the breaking away from European tradition that was to produce types like the American whaler, frigate, and clipper ship.

Pl. 103. Another snow-rigged vessel with a ship-like hull; one of the earliest of American models. Unlike the Danish snow, this has a boom.

Pl. 104. This shows the latest 18th-century fashions. The stem is less raking and the beak-head lighter and smaller. The decoration is slight, but there is still considerable sheer, though the wales have grown inconspicuous. A boom on the mizen is a conspicuous new feature. There is also now a flying jib-boom, at first a separate spar.

Pl. 105. Here as in the last ship the wales are less conspicuous, and the channels are all at one level. Ironwork has come into use for nettings. There is no dolphin-striker, and a mizenyard is still carried.

Pl. 106. The *bootschip*, "boatship," is a descendant of the old flight, Plates 20 and 40. These vessels were sometimes built round up to the top of the stern, making them into ship-rigged galliots. Dutch whalers were of this build, with just such little windows in the stern cheeks. The windlass is seen just abaft the foremast, which is further forward than in modern ships. Old fashions survive in the "ass-head" caps with ties still running over them to "ram-head" blocks. The sail plan is still that of fifty years before, and the spritsail-topmast knee is seen on the bowsprit. Such round-sterned Dutch vessels were still extant after the middle of the 19th century.

Pl. 107. This has been thought to have been made by a prisoner of war in 1779, but the rig will scarcely allow of it; 1812 seems more likely if it is an American war-prisoner's work. It is a fine specimen of the unprofessional model. The curve of the rails of the head is at last destroyed here with a straight rail, and we see a mizen-topgallantsail for the first time set.

Pl. 108. The "pinkship" of the Baltic, like the English pinks, was originally round-sterned in imitation of Dutch fashions. The stern here is more like the square tuck still seen on Danish coasters with its davits. The "pinkship" is distinguished from the "frigate-ship" especially by its lack of a mizen topgallant-sail. Here the other topgallants and the royals are rigged in polacca style, both coming down together when furled.

Pl. 109. An example of the large class of bone "prisoner's models," this one is very highly finished; the crowfoot to the mizen gaff is rather typical of their involved work. Another "extra" is the "sprit-topgallantsail." The double dolphin-striker of the time is well seen here. The black bands on the hull are not usual on such bone models. Boats are added; one hanging at davits astern.

Pl. 110. The lessened rake of the stern, and the very slight sheer show early signs of the 19th century; the waist, however, is still open, and the beak-head except for the straightened upper rail, is of the old pattern. Boat-davits are fitted astern only.

Pl. 111. French and English ships are changing together. The lower poop, and the mizen channels in line with the others distinguish this from the *Hero* of Plate 110. The sails, hammocks, and awnings are all shown drying, and one of the ship's boats with sails is also seen. The spritsail and spritsail-topsail are still carried.

Pl. 112. The davits on the quarter, if original, would put this ship further on. The quarter gallery and the head, with the marked sheer aft, seem early features, and so does the short jib-boom.

Pl. 113. A block model, not carved to scale, but interesting as showing the American frigate type—a very much more powerful ship than a frigate of Europe. The beakhead-bulkhead has now disappeared, the bows being brought up round behind the beak, and the head-rails topped with a head-board, carrying the straightness of the rest of the hull right forward.

Pl. 114. Bomb-ketches had at their origin been round-sterned and Dutch-built; hence the French name *galiote à bombes*. This one carried 2 mortars and 8 guns. The rig derives from small hooker-like coasters, and had been used in England for yachts also. It is practically that of a foremastless ship.

Pl. 115. The early cutter, like this one, was usually clinker-built. Her rig derives in part from that of the hoy, Plate 69, but she is given a running bow-sprit and a "brigantine" mainsail that lowers and has a boom. The stay in older cutters is always set up to the stem-head as in the hoy; the dead-eye being turned in "cutter-stay-fashion," leaving room for the sail to run down close to the stem when lowered. Very fast boats, these had to contend with cutters and luggers of the "Smuggling Service" that were often faster still, and as well armed.

Pl. 116. This shows, below, the finer lines introduced by Sir W. Symonds. The rounded bow, covered waist, and straight head-board are new since the *Hero*, Plate 110; so are the boat davits on the quarters, and the trysail gaffs on the fore and main masts. The spritsail-topgallant sail is seen no more, and the spritsail itself is rarely set. The cradle for launching is seen alongside.

Pl. 117. Showing a reluctance of French builders to adopt the new sea-fashions, in build and rig *L'Hercule* resembles the *Hero*, Plate 110, rather than the *Vanguard*, Plate 116, keeping the square beakhead and carved head-rails, and also the deep waist. She has no quarter-davits, and keeps her spritsail-topsail yard and top crowfeet, given up in the English ship.

Pl. 118. A "Symondite" brig, this has the sharper build introduced by Sir W. Symonds; as here rigged it shows the "spritsail gaffs" on the bowsprit. The similar training brigs, useful as giving instruction in square rig on a small two-masted vessel, were the last representatives of sail in the British Navy.

Pl. 119. A rough, disproportionate block model, but of an interesting type. The American whaler has travelled a long way from the flight-built Dutch *Walvischvaarder* that set the fashion for 18th-century English and other whalers. Another whaler model at New Bedford is enormous, being built half the size of the original. It was on whalers that the old wide channels were first abandoned as being in the way of the boats. This model is without channels; those of the large model are narrow and are protected by skids. The fiddle-head takes the place of a sculpture, and plainness is the prevailing note. The flying jib-boom is still a separate spar. The double dolphin striker serves as " spritsail gaffs " as well.

Pl. 120. This is still more a " frigate-ship " than a true " clipper," but shows fine lines with a good deal of American influence. The narrow channels are placed high, the foremast has travelled back from the bows, a " monkey-gaff " is carried and outriggers spread the backstays at the topmast crosstrees. No sail is as yet carried on the cro'jack yard. The fore braces now lead down to the sides; no longer to the main stay.

Pl. 121. Something of a freak when built, this fine McKay clipper has the four-masted barque rig that is now typical of the big merchant ship. Her double topsails are of the original pattern, the lower topsail having two reefs and being larger than the upper one. She has the typical sheering bows of the American clipper, and the masts are more gracefully varied in height than in her successors. The deck-houses, somewhat resembling contemporary railway carriages, are conspicuous recent additions to the sailing ship.

Pl. 122. The double topsails are now of the modern kind, the lower topsail yard being fixed at the cap. The mizen topsail is still single, but a sail would be carried on the cro'jack yard. The mizen is fitted snow-fashion, with a little snow-mast, and a monkey-gaff carries the " Stars and Stripes." The deck-houses, and most other details of the hull, including the double channels, are just as they remained in American ships of the " eighties " and " nineties " and have set the fashions to a great extent for all later merchant ships. English clippers were by no means a mere imitation of these American ships; but the type, originating in America, is perhaps best represented by a ship such as this.

Pl. 123. The hull is of wood, but with iron beams. The nearly upright stem, flat sides, turtle-back poop, and round stern also suggest iron construction and steam. The bowsprit and the spars generally are somewhat stumpy as compared with those of a clipper, though many of her features are derived from such ships.

Pl. 124. The steel four-masted barque represents the last, perhaps the very last, word in square-rig. Double topgallant yards are now carried as well as double topsail yards, saving trouble but adding to the monotonous effect given by the repetition of detail on each mast. The hull keeps some of the sheer of the clipper, but its extreme length makes the stump bowsprit seem even shorter than it is. Ventilators aft, anchor davits forward, and a donkey-engine amidships all suggest steam; but this ship has not adopted the auxiliary steam or motor propulsion that we find in some that are still newer. The present tendency is towards a simplified schooner rig and auxiliary motor power, which, to judge by the history of steam, is likely to end in another victory of mechanism over sails, cheapness being gained by saving on man-power what is spent on fuel.

78

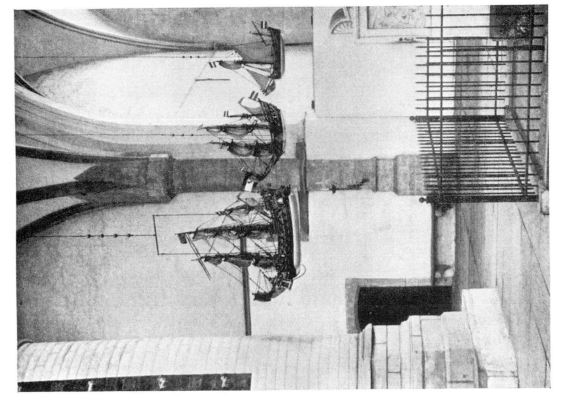

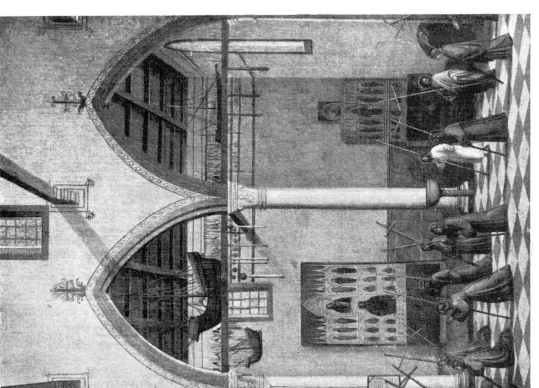

PLATE 1.

DETAIL OF CARPACCIO'S "PROCESSION IN A CHURCH,"
SHOWING VOTIVE "CHURCH-SHIPS"
(R. Academy of Fine Arts, Venice; Photo, Alinari)

INTERIOR OF THE GROOTE KERK, HAARLEM, WITH
COMMEMORATIVE "CHURCH-SHIPS."

PLATE 2.
GOLD CUP, 1503, FOUNDED ON THE "KRAECK" OF W A
(Germanic National Museum, Nuremberg)

PLATE 3.
THE "GREAT MICHAEL," 1511. MODEL EXECUTED BY
MR. R. PATTERSON
(On exhibition at the Royal Museum, Edinburgh)

PLATE 4.
MODEL OF UNKNOWN ORIGIN, BUT APPARENTLY A
" CHURCH-SHIP " OF *circa* 1525
(*In the Collection of the late Sir William Van Horne*)

PLATE 5.
VENETIAN "CHURCH-SHIP" OF MIDDLE OF XVITH CENTURY
(Museo Storico Navale, Venice)

PLATE 6.
FRENCH GALLEON XVITH CENTURY
HANGING MODEL MADE BY R. MORTON NANCE
(*In the possession of R. W. Mackenzie, Esq.*)

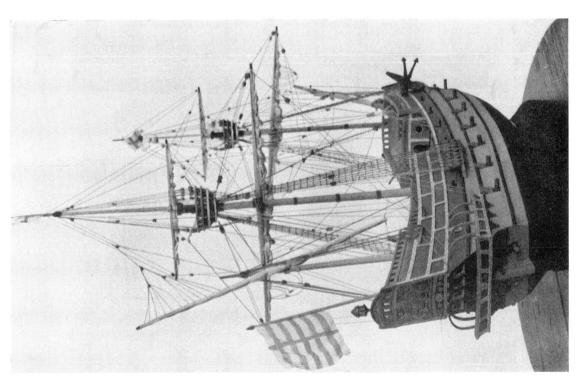

PLATE 7.
ELIZABETHAN SHIP, 1590-1600
MODEL MADE BY R. MORTON NANCE
(In the possession of Colonel Gascoigne)

PLATE 8.
LATE XVITH CENTURY "CHURCH-SHIP," WITH MONOGRAM OF
CHRISTIAN IV. OF DENMARK ON STERN. RE-RIGGED
circa 1720.
(*Trinity House, Leith, Scotland*)

PLATE 9.

FLEMISH MODEL OF GALLEON, END OF XVITH CENTURY

(Museo Naval, Madrid)

PLATE 10.
FLEMISH MODEL OF GALLEON, END OF XVIth CENTURY.
FROM AN OLDER PHOTOGRAPH SHOWING DECORATION
(Museo Naval, Madrid)

PLATE 11.
" CHURCH-SHIP " WITH PAINTED SAILS, DATED 1603
(Germanic National Museum, Nuremberg)

PLATE 12.
HUDSON'S " HALVE MAEN " (HALF MOON), 1609. MODEL
CONSTRUCTED BY MR. C. G. E. CRONE, AMSTERDAM.

PLATE 13.
HUDSON'S "HALVE MAEN" (HALF MOON), 1609.   MODEL
CONSTRUCTED BY MR. C. G. E. CRONE

PLATE 14.
" Church-Ship," *circa* 1610. St. Mary's Church, Bergen

PLATE 15.

" CHURCH-SHIP," *circa* 1620. GROOTE KERK, HAARLEM

BREMEN, *circa* 1620.

BREMEN, *circa* 1645.

BREMEN, *circa* 1790.

EMDEN, *circa* 1700.

PLATE 16.
TOWN HALL HANGING MODELS OF "CHURCH-SHIP" TYPE
in situ

PLATE 17.
THE "SOVERAIGNE OF THE SEAS," 1637. MODEL
CONSTRUCTED BY MR. HENRY B. CULVER, NEW YORK

PLATE 18.

BOW OF THE "SOVERAIGNE OF THE SEAS," 1637. MODEL
CONSTRUCTED BY MR. HENRY B. CULVER

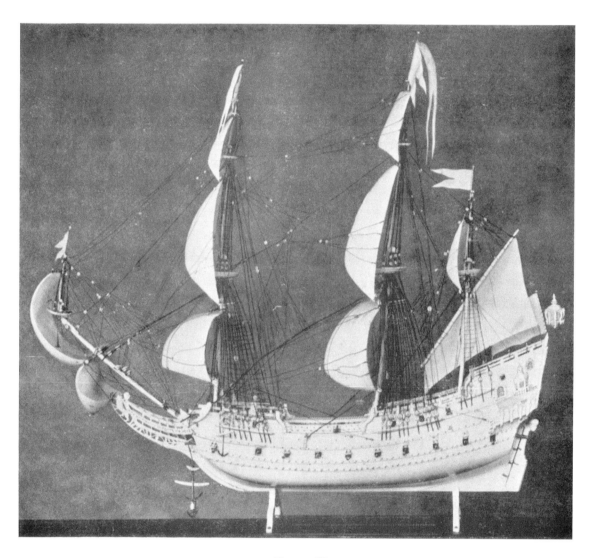

PLATE 19.
THE "NORSKE LÖVE" (NORSE LION), 1634
IVORY MODEL CARVED BY JAKOB JENSEN, 1654
(Rosenborg Castle, Copenhagen)

PLATE 20.
DUTCH FLIGHT, *circa* 1645
(Nederlandsch Historisch Scheepvaart Museum, Amsterdam)

PLATE 21.
DUTCH EAST INDIAMAN, "PRINS WILLEM," 1651
(*Nederlandsch Historisch Scheepvaart Museum, Amsterdam*)

PLATE 22.
THE "AMARANTHE," 1654. REPLICA OF ORIGINAL MODEL IN
THE STATE COLLECTION, STOCKHOLM
(*Maritime Museum, Gothenburg*)

PLATE 23.

STERN OF DUTCH MAN-OF-WAR, *circa* 1660

(Hohenzollern Museum, Berlin)

PLATE 24.
DUTCH MAN-OF-WAR, *circa* 1660
(Hohenzollern Museum, Berlin)

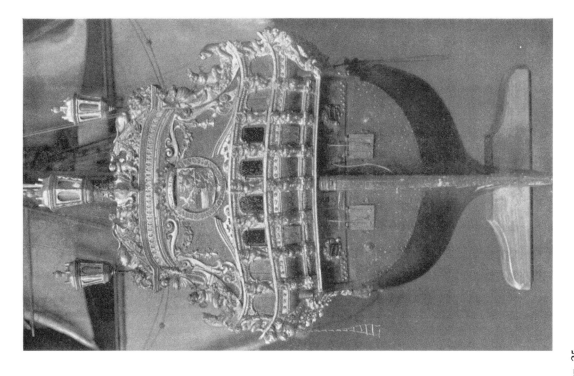

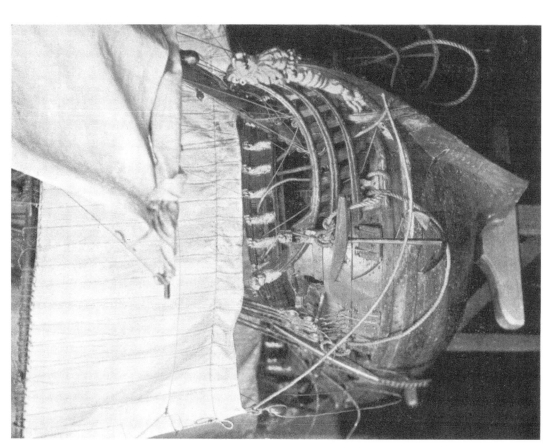

PLATE 25.

DUTCH MAN-OF-WAR, circa 1660 : BOW AND STERN

(Hohenzollern Museum, Berlin)

PLATE 26.

HANGING "CHURCH-SHIP" TYPE MODEL
OF ARMED SHIP, *circa* 1660.
FROM A DRAWING BY R. MORTON NANCE.

(Hall of the Schiffergesellschaft, Lübeck.)

PLATE 27.
THE "ZEELANDIA," FLAGSHIP OF ADMIRAL JAN
EVERTSZEN, 1662
("Prins Hendrik" Maritime Museum, Rotterdam)

PLATE 28.
DUTCH MAN-OF-WAR " HOLLANDIA," 82 GUNS, 1665-1683
(*Nederlandsch Historisch Scheepvaart Museum, Amsterdam*)

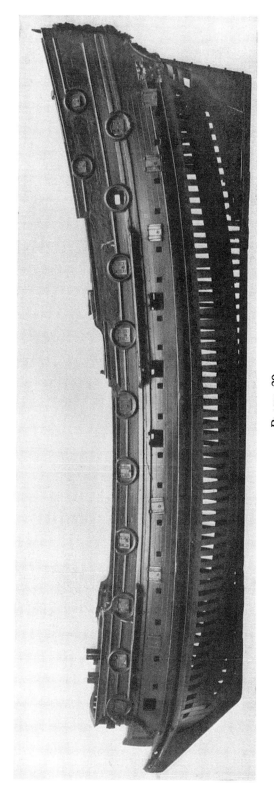

PLATE 29.
THE "BRISTOL," 1666; REBUILT DEPTFORD, 1693.
(Royal Naval Museum, Greenwich)

PLATE 30.
ENGLISH 90-GUN SHIP, PROBABLY THE "CHARLES" OF 1668.
RIGGED BY R. C. ANDERSON.
(In the possession of R. C. Anderson, Esq.)

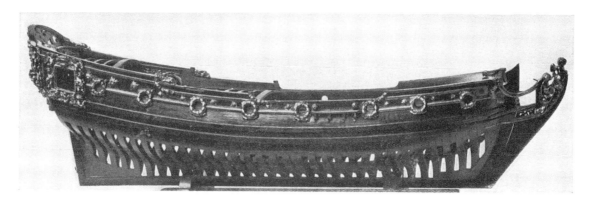

PLATE 31.
BOW OF 100-GUN SHIP, *circa* 1670
(In the Collection of the Training Ship "Mercury")
ENGLISH YACHT, *circa* 1670-1700
(In the possession of R. C. Anderson, Esq.)

PLATE 32.
THE "PRINCE," FIRST-RATE LINE-OF-BATTLE SHIP, BUILT AT
CHATHAM, 1670, BY PHINEAS PETT. RIGGING NOT ORIGINAL
(Science Museum, South Kensington)

PLATE 33.
ENGLISH ADMIRALTY YACHT, " THE NAVY," 1672.
(Metropolitan Museum, New York; lent by Colonel H. H. Rogers.
Formerly in the Cuckfield Collection)

PLATE 34.
DANISH THREE-DECKER, "CHRISTIANUS QUINTUS," 1673
MODERN MODEL
(*Danish Admiralty, Copenhagen*)

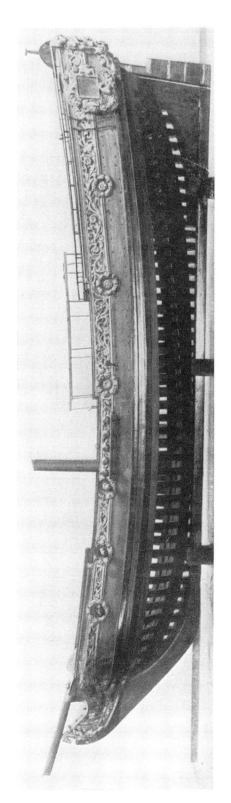

PLATE 35.

THE "ALBERMARLE," 90 GUNS, BUILT 1680
(Royal United Service Museum)

ENGLISH ROYAL YACHT, circa 1680
(In the Collection of the Training Ship "Mercury")

PLATE 36.
" DIE HOFFNUNG " (THE HOPE), LÜBECK SHIP OF *circa* 1680.
CONTEMPORARY MODEL WITH LATER REPAIRS
(*Museum für Kunst-und Kulturgeschichte, Lübeck*)

PLATE 37.
THE " CORONATION," 90 GUNS, 1686. RIGGED BY
R. C. ANDERSON AND L. A. PRITCHARD.
(*Formerly in the London Museum*)

PLATE 38.
DANISH TWO-DECKER "CHURCH-SHIP," LATE XVIIth
CENTURY, WITH XIXth CENTURY RENOVATIONS
(Kunstgewerbe Museum, Flensburg)

PLATE 39.
DUTCH 90-GUN SHIP, *circa* 1685. RIGGED BY
R. C. ANDERSON.
(In the possession of R. C. Anderson, Esq.)

PLATE 40.

HANGING "CHURCH-SHIP" TYPE MODEL OF
A LÜBECK FLIGHT, DATED 1690 ON STERN,
BUT WITH XVIIITH CENTURY JIB-BOOM.
FROM A DRAWING BY R. MORTON NANCE.

(Hall of the Schiffergesellschaft, Lübeck.)

PLATE 41.
NORWEGIAN "CHURCH-SHIP," WITH LEGEND "DEN
FORGYLTE SVAN (THE GILDED SWAN), ANNO 1691"
ON STERN. RIGGING PARTLY CONTEMPORARY
(*Bergens Museum, Bergen*)

PLATE 42.
FRENCH LINE-OF-BATTLESHIP, "LE ROYAL-LOUIS," 1692
(Musée de Marine, Paris)

PLATE 43.
ENGLISH 50-GUN SHIP, 1695
(Metropolitan Museum, New York; lent by Colonel H. H. Rogers.
Formerly in the Cuckfield Collection)

PLATE 44.
ENGLISH 80-GUN SHIP, 1695.
(Metropolitan Museum, New York; lent by Colonel H. H. Rogers
Formerly in the Cuckfield Collection)

PLATE 45.

MODEL OF "L'AGRÉABLE", FRENCH TWO-DECKER, 1695.
FROM A DRAWING BY R. MORTON NANCE.

(Musée de Marine, Paris.)

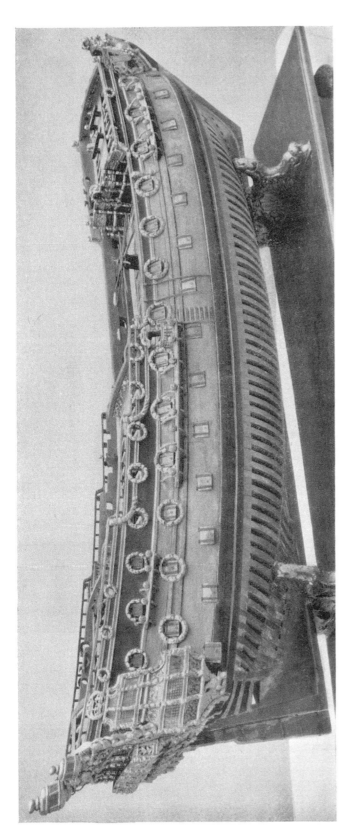

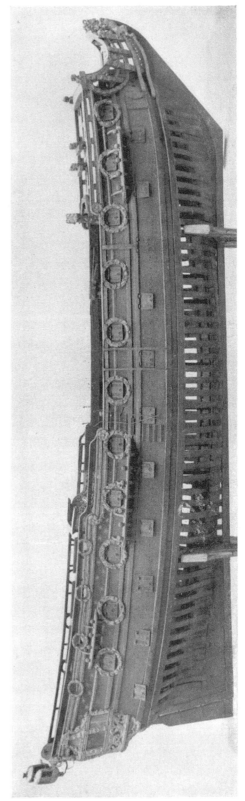

PLATE 46.
ENGLISH 80-GUN SHIP, *circa* 1695.
ENGLISH 50-GUN SHIP, DATED 1703
(Metropolitan Museum, New York; lent by Colonel H. H. Rogers.
Formerly in the Cuckfield Collection)

PLATE 47.
DANISH FRIGATE OF THE TIME OF TORDENSKJOLD (1691-1720)
(Kronborg Museum, Elsinore)

PLATE 48.
NORWEGIAN "CHURCH-SHIP," END OF XVIITH CENTURY,
WITH ORIGINAL RIGGING
(*Bergens Museum, Bergen*)

PLATE 49.
GENOESE " CHURCH-SHIP," END OF XVIITH CENTURY, WITH
ORIGINAL RIGGING
(Palazzo Bianco, Genoa)

PLATE 50.

"DER LÖWE" (THE LION). ARMED FLIGHT, "CHURCH SHIP"
MODEL. LATE XVIITH CENTURY

(Museum für Kunst-und Kulturgeschichte, Lübeck)

PLATE 51.
"LA RÉALE," FRENCH "ADMIRAL GALLEY," 1690-1715
VENETIAN TRADING GALEASS, DATED 1726
(Musée de Marine, Paris)

PLATE 52.
GENOESE GALLEY, END OF XVIITH CENTURY
(Palazzo Bianco, Genoa)

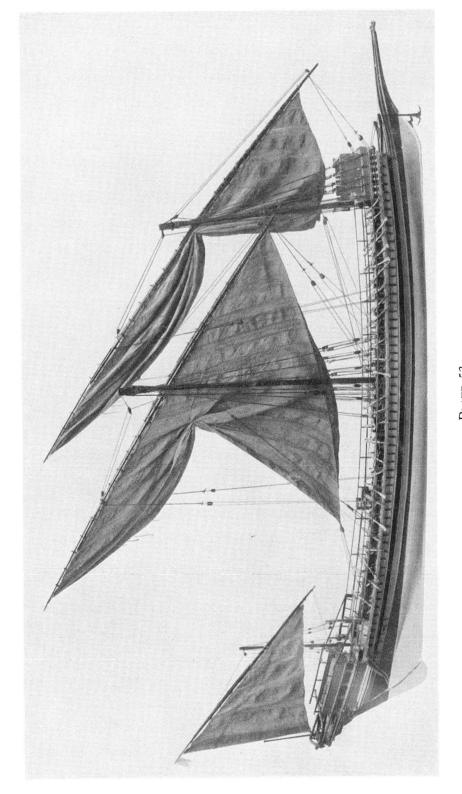

PLATE 53.

MALTESE GALLEY, FIRST HALF OF XVIIIth CENTURY

*(Royal Naval Museum, Greenwich; presented by the
Duke of Northumberland, 1828)*

PLATE 54.

ENGLISH 50-GUN SHIP, 1690-1700

(Royal Naval Museum, Greenwich)

PLATE 55.
ENGLISH 50-GUN SHIP, *circa* 1700
(*Metropolitan Museum, New York; lent by Colonel H. H. Rogers.*
Formerly in the Cuckfield Collection)

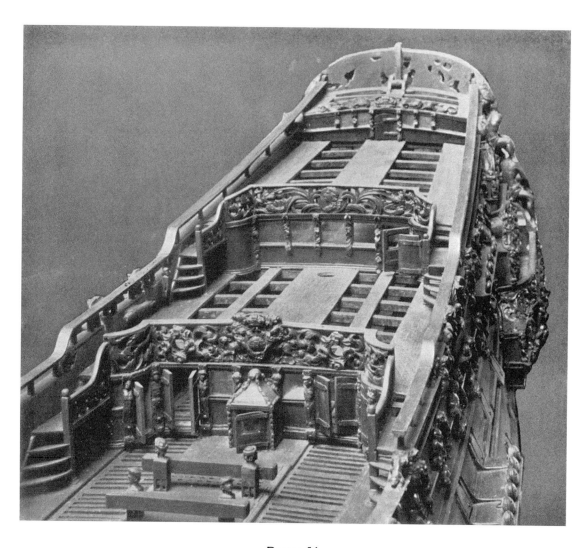

PLATE 56.
DECKS OF THE "BRITANNIA," 1700
(Metropolitan Museum, New York; lent by Colonel H. H. Rogers.
Formerly in the Cuckfield Collection)

PLATE 57.
DETAILS OF STERN AND BOW OF THE "BRITANNIA," 1700
(Metropolitan Museum, New York; lent by Colonel H. H. Rogers.
Formerly in the Cuckfield Collection)

PLATE 58.
THE "ST. GEORGE," SECOND-RATE, 96 GUNS, 1701
(Metropolitan Museum, New York; lent by Colonel H. H. Rogers.
Formerly in the Cuckfield Collection)

PLATE 59.
STERN OF THE " ST. GEORGE," 1701
(Metropolitan Museum, New York; lent by Colonel H. H. Rogers.
Formerly in the Cuckfield Collection)

PLATE 60.
THE "ST. GEORGE," 1701. DETAILS OF BOW AND MAIN-TOP,
ETC.
(*Metropolitan Museum, New York; lent by Colonel H. H. Rogers.*
Formerly in the Cuckfield Collection)

PLATE 61.
SWEDISH "CHURCH-SHIP," EARLY XVIIITH CENTURY
(Maritime Museum, Gothenburg)

PLATE 62.
THE " MARLBOROUGH," 90 GUNS, 1708. RIGGED BY
R. C. ANDERSON
(Formerly in the London Museum)

PLATE 63.

ENGLISH 60-GUN SHIP, BEGINNING OF XVIIITH CENTURY.
RESTORED AND RIGGED BY MR. H. B. CULVER

(In the Collection of Col. H. H. Rogers)

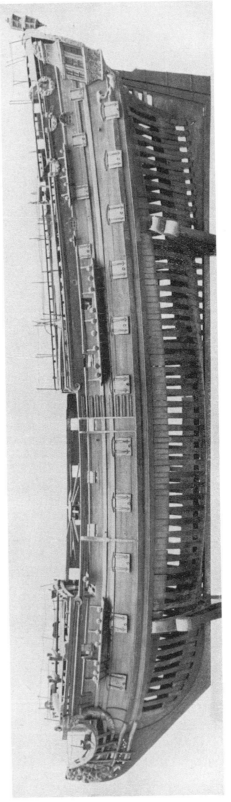

PLATE 64.
ENGLISH 70-GUN SHIP, 1710
ENGLISH 54-GUN SHIP circa 1710
(Metropolitan Museum, New York; lent by Colonel H. H. Rogers
Formerly in the Cuckfield Collection)

PLATE 65.

STERNS OF ENGLISH 50-GUN SHIP OF 1703; ENGLISH 60-GUN
SHIP OF BEGINNING OF XVIIITH CENTURY; AND ENGLISH
54-GUN SHIP OF 1710

(Metropolitan Museum, New York, lent by Colonel H. H. Rogers.
Formerly in the Cuckfield Collection)

PLATE 66.

SMALL ENGLISH VESSEL, PROBABLY A SNOW, *circa* 1710

(In the possession of R. C. Anderson, Esq.)

THE "CAROLINA," 1710-1716

(In the Collection of the Training Ship "Mercury")

PLATE 67.
ENGLISH SHIP, PROBABLY THE " ROYAL GEORGE," 1715.
(*Technische Hochschule, Hanover; Photo Max Baumann*)

PLATE 68.
STERN OF ENGLISH SHIP, PROBABLY THE "ROYAL GEORGE,"
1715
(*Technische Hochschule, Hanover; Photo, Max Baumann*)

PLATE 69.
ENGLISH HOY, 1700-1730. MODEL MADE BY
R. MORTON NANCE
(On Exhibition at the Science Museum, South Kensington)

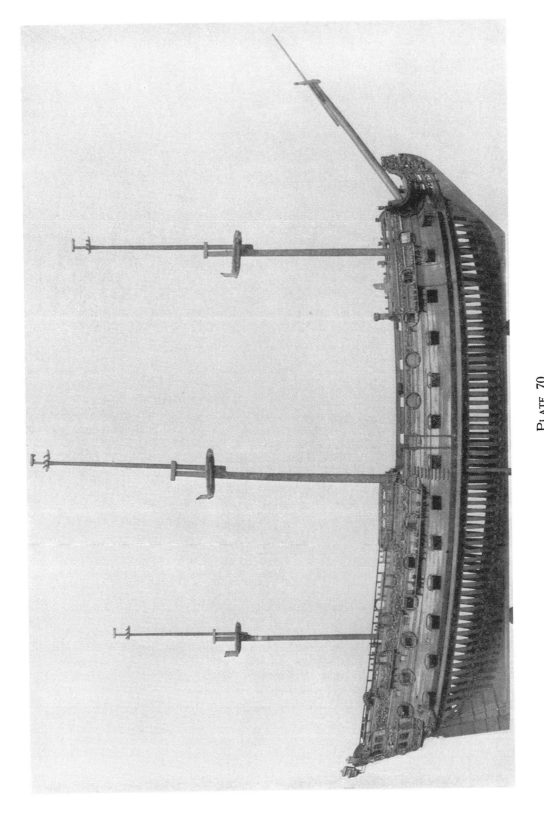

PLATE 70.

ENGLISH FOURTH-RATE MAN-OF-WAR, 60 GUNS
BUILT ABOUT 1715 ON THE ESTABLISHMENT OF 1706
(Science Museum, South Kensington; lent by H. J. Dafforne, Esq.)

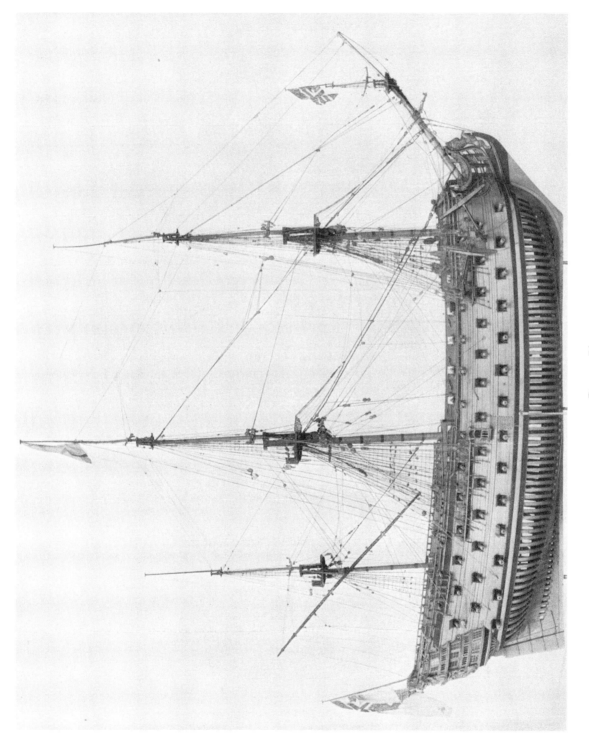

PLATE 71.
ENGLISH THIRD-RATE LINE-OF-BATTLE SHIP,
1719 ESTABLISHMENT
(Science Museum, South Kensington; lent by executors of
Mrs. Humphry)

PLATE 72.
THE "ROYAL WILLIAM," 100 GUNS. BUILT 1682;
RE-BUILT 1692 AND 1719
(*Metropolitan Museum, New York; lent by Colonel H. H. Rogers.
Formerly in the Cuckfield Collection*)

Plate 73.
The "Royal William," 100 Guns. Built 1682;
Re-built 1692 and 1719
(Royal Naval Museum, Greenwich)

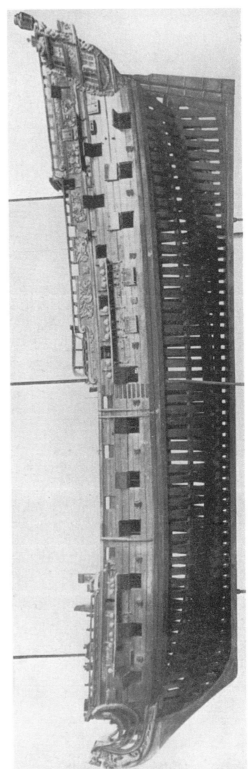

PLATE 74.

ENGLISH 70-GUN SHIP, circa 1720
(In the possession of R. C. Anderson, Esq.)

ENGLISH 60-GUN SHIP, circa 1720. FITTED FOR SWEEPS
(In the Collection of the Training Ship "Mercury")

PLATE 75.
DUTCH EAST INDIAMAN, "DEN ARY," 54 GUNS, 1725
(Nederlandsch Historisch Scheepvaart Museum, Amsterdam)

PLATE 76.
ENGLISH THIRD-RATE LINE-OF-BATTLESHIP,
EARLY XVIIIth CENTURY
(Science Museum, South Kensington; lent by P. E. D. Hammond, Esq.)

PLATE 77.

ADMIRAL SIR JOHN BALCHEN'S "VICTORY," 1737 (WRECKED
ON THE CASQUETS, SEPTEMBER, 1744)

(Royal Naval Museum, Greenwich)

PLATE 78.
THE " FLORA," SPANISH 26-GUN FRIGATE BUILT AT GUERNECA,
1739
(Museo Naval, Madrid)

PLATE 79.
PRIVATEER " NEPTUNUS." MODERN MODEL FROM PLANS BY
CHAPMAN
(*Maritime Museum, Gothenburg*)

PLATE 80.
DUTCH EAST INDIAMAN, *circa* 1740
(*Nederlandsch Historisch Scheepvaart Museum, Amsterdam*)

PLATE 81.

MODEL OF A DUTCH SHIP *circa* 1740.
FROM A DRAWING BY R. MORTON NANCE.

(Musée de Marine, Paris.)

PLATE 82.
ENGLISH MAN-OF-WAR, FOURTH-RATE, 1740-1745
(Science Museum, South Kensington)

PLATE 83.
DANISH 50-GUN SHIP " FYN," 1746
(Danish Admiralty, Copenhagen)

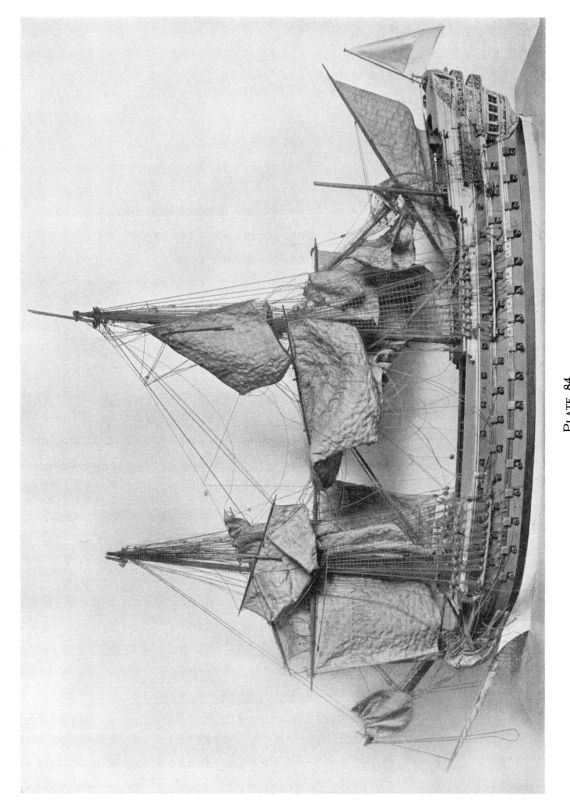

PLATE 84.

FRENCH LINE-OF-BATTLE SHIP, "LE BIEN-AIMÉ,"
PERIOD OF LOUIS XV.
(Musée de Marine, Paris)

PLATE 85.

SPANISH TWO-DECKER, FIRST HALF OF XVIIIth CENTURY,
SHOWN AS LAID UP FOR THE WINTER

(*Museo Naval, Madrid*)

PLATE 86.
DUTCH EAST INDIAMAN, "DE JONKVROUW CATHARINA
CORNELIA." MIDDLE OF XVIIITH CENTURY
("Prins Hendrik" Maritime Museum, Rotterdam)

PLATE 87.
ENGLISH FRIGATE, 24 GUNS, BUILT *circa* 1750
(Science Museum, South Kensington)

PLATE 88.
SWEDISH EAST INDIAMAN, 1750
(*Maritime Museum, Gothenburg*)

PLATE 89.
DUTCH ADMIRALTY YACHT, *circa* 1750
(Nederlandsch Historisch Scheepvaart Museum, Amsterdam)

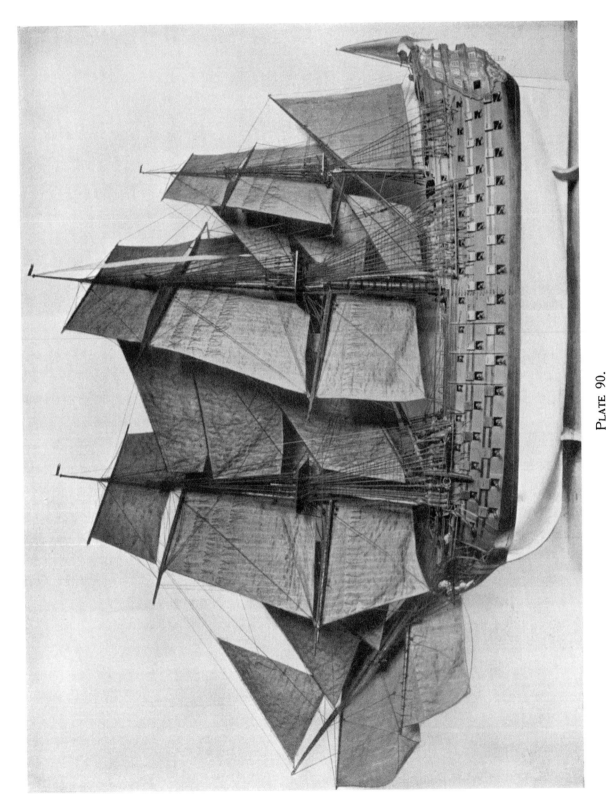

PLATE 90.

FRENCH LINE-OF-BATTLE SHIP, "LE SANS-PAREIL,"
108 GUNS, 1760

(Musée de Marine, Paris)

PLATE 91.
FRENCH FRIGATE, PERIOD OF LOUIS XVI.
(Musée de Marine, Paris)

PLATE 92.
FRENCH LUGGER, "LE COUREUR," 8 GUNS, 1775
(Musée de Marine, Paris)

PLATE 93.
FRENCH LINE-OF-BATTLE SHIP "L'ARTÉSIEN,"
64 GUNS, 1774-1786
(Musée de Marine, Paris)

PLATE 94.
SWEDISH ROYAL YACHT "AMPHION," BUILT BY
CHAPMAN, 1779
(State Naval-History Collections, Stockholm)

PLATE 95.
DUTCH MERCHANTMAN, " RUST EN WERK "
(REST AND WORK), 1780
("Prins Hendrik" Maritime Museum, Rotterdam)

PLATE 96.
ENGLISH SLOOP OF WAR, SCHOONER RIGGED, *circa* 1780
(Science Museum, South Kensington)

PLATE 97.
DUTCH FRIGATE, " WAGENINGEN," *circa* 1780
(Musée de Marine, Paris)

PLATE 98.
ENGLISH 64-GUN SHIP, PERIOD 1780-1790
(Science Museum, South Kensington)

PLATE 99.
SPANISH CHEBEC OF THE TYPE BUILT FOR ATTACKING
THE FORTIFICATIONS OF ALGIERS, 1783
(Museo Naval, Madrid)

PLATE 100.
SPANISH THREE-DECKER " REAL CARLOS," BUILT AT
HAVANA, 1787
(*Museo Naval, Madrid*)

PLATE 101.
" DIE VERÄNDERUNG " (THE CHANGE). FLENSBURG
TRADING SNOW OF 1794. RECONSTRUCTION
(Altonaer Museum, Altona)

PLATE 102.
AMERICAN MERCHANTMAN, "ARM AND HOPE," BUILT
PROVIDENCE, R.I., 1796
(In the possession of Mr. Clarkson A. Collins, Jr., New York)

PLATE 103.

SNOW "RISING STATES," LATE XVIIITH CENTURY

(*Peabody Museum of Salem, Mass.*)

PLATE 104.
H.M.S. "AJAX," 74-GUN LINE-OF-BATTLE SHIP BUILT AT
ROTHERHITHE, 1795-1798
(Science Museum, South Kensington)

PLATE 105.
DUTCH LINE-OF-BATTLE SHIP, "CHATTAM,"
76 GUNS, 1800
(Nederlandsch Historisch Scheepvaart Museum. Amsterdam)

PLATE 106.
DUTCH BOOTSHIP, "DE GOEDE HOOP" (GOOD HOPE),
END OF XVIIIth CENTURY
(Nederlandsch Historisch Scheepvaart Museum, Amsterdam)

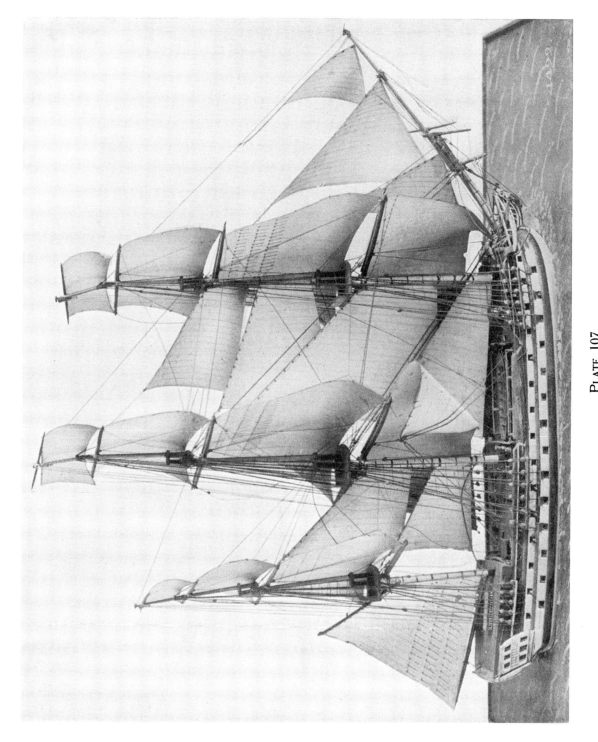

PLATE 107.
MODEL OF TWO-DECKER MADE BY AN AMERICAN
PRISONER OF WAR IN ENGLAND, 1779
(Peabody Museum of Salem, Mass.)

PLATE 108.
PINKSHIP-RIGGED WEST INDIAMAN, "DORIS."
FLENSBURG, 1800. RECONSTRUCTION
(*Altonaer Museum, Altona*)

PLATE 109.
ENGLISH FRIGATE "AEOLUS," 1801. BONE "PRISONER'S"
MODEL
(Science Museum, South Kensington)

PLATE 110.

H.M.S. "HERO," THIRD-RATE LINE-OF-BATTLE SHIP,
74 GUNS, BUILT ON THE THAMES 1803, RIGGING BY
J. T. MAJOR, 1921

(Science Museum, South Kensington; lent by Sir Alan H. Moore, Bart.)

PLATE 111.
FRENCH LINE-OF-BATTLE SHIP, "L'ACHILLE," 1803
(Musée de Marine, Paris)

PLATE 112.
DANISH CORVETTE, EARLY XIXTH CENTURY
(Kronberg Museum, Elsinore)

PLATE 113.
PRIVATEER "AMERICA," OF THE WAR OF 1812,
BUILT AT SALEM
(*Peabody Museum of Salem, Mass.*)

PLATE 114.

FRENCH BOMB-KETCH, 8 GUNS AND 2 MORTARS, 1815

(Musée de Marine, Paris)

PLATE 115.
REVENUE CUTTER, 14 GUNS, 1810-1830
(Science Museum, South Kensington)

PLATE 116.
H.M.S. "VANGUARD," 80-GUN TWO-DECKER BUILT AT
PEMBROKE, 1835
(Science Museum, South Kensington)

PLATE 117.

FRENCH 80-GUN SHIP "L'HERCULE," 1835

(In the possession of Mons. Jacques Sottas, Paris)

Plate 118.
H.M.S. "Fantôme," Brig-Rigged Sloop-of-War,
Launched at Chatham, 1839
(*Science Museum, South Kensington*)

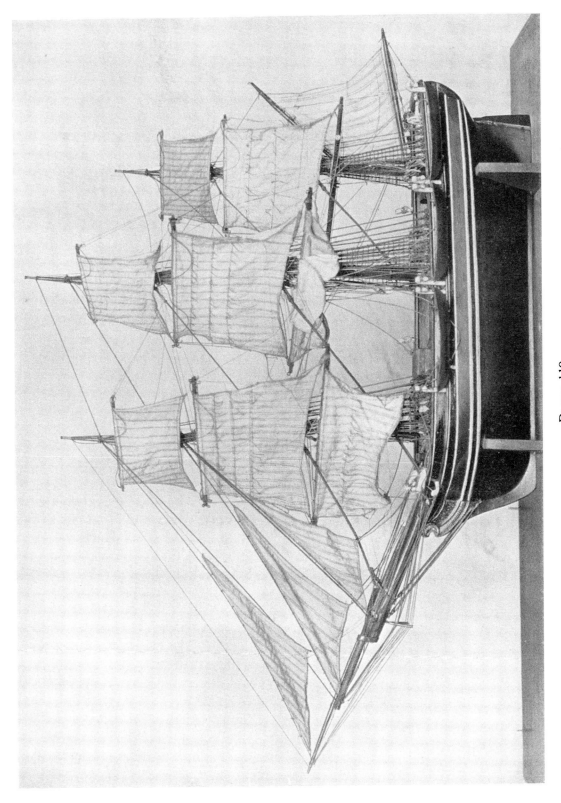

PLATE 119.
AMERICAN WHALER, *circa* 1850
(*Old Dartmouth Historical Society, New Bedford, Mass.*)

PLATE 120.
THE "JAVA," CLIPPER TYPE MERCHANTMAN BUILT AT
HAMBURG, 1852
(Altonaer Museum, Altona)

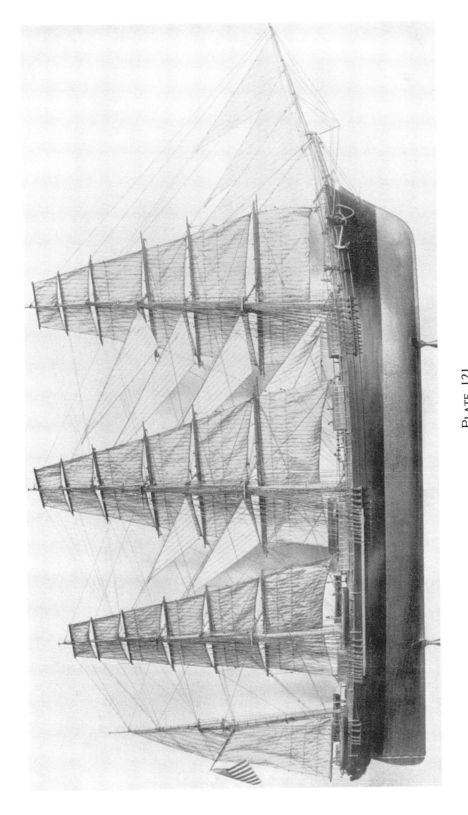

PLATE 121.

THE "GREAT REPUBLIC," AMERICAN CLIPPER, BUILT AT
BOSTON, MASS., 1853
(Musée de Marine, Paris)

PLATE 122.
THE "YOUNG AMERICA," BUILT AT NEW YORK, 1853.
BY WILLIAM H. WEBB
(Formerly in the Carlton Chapman Collection)

PLATE 123.
MERCHANT SHIP "CARMARTHENSHIRE," 1865
(Science Museum, South Kensington)

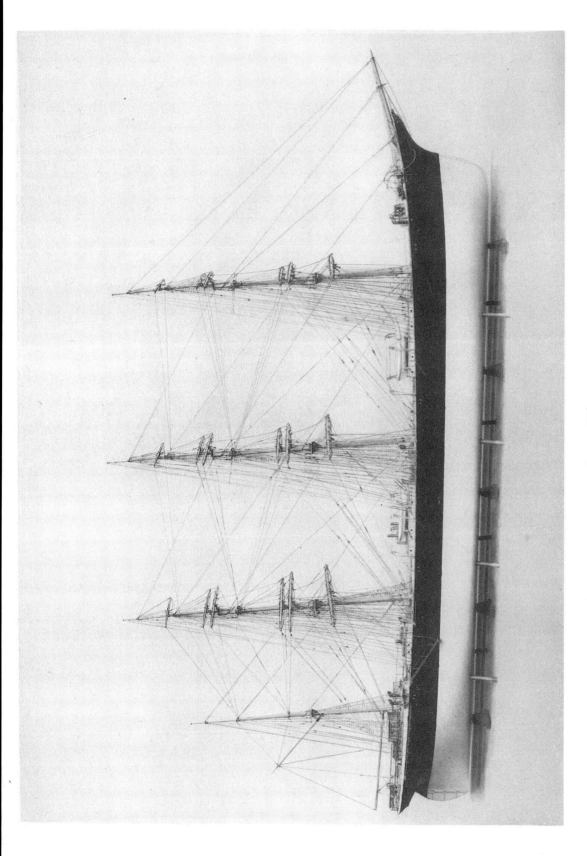

PLATE 124.

THE "CALIFORNIA," LAST WHITE STAR SAILING CLIPPER,
BUILT AT BELFAST 1890

(Science Museum, South Kensington; lent by the Oceanic Steam
Navigation Company, Ltd.)